Graduate's Guide

Mazen Kavvas

Graduate's Guide

Bibliographic Information published by the
Deutsche Nationalbibliothek
The Deutsche Nationalbibliothek lists this publication in the Deutsche Nationalbibliografie; detailed bibliographic data is available online at http://dnb.d-nb.de.

Library of Congress Cataloging-in-Publication Data
A CIP catalog record for this book has been applied for at the Library of Congress.

Cover illustration: © alluranet/istockphoto.com

ISBN 978-3-631-85451-8 (Print)
E-ISBN 978-3-631-85524-9 (E-PDF)
E-ISBN 978-3-631-85739-7 (EPUB)
DOI 10.3726/b18536

© Peter Lang GmbH
Internationaler Verlag der Wissenschaften
Berlin 2022
All rights reserved.

Peter Lang – Berlin · Bern · Bruxelles · New York · Istanbul · Oxford · Warszawa · Wien

All parts of this publication are protected by copyright. Any utilisation outside the strict limits of the copyright law, without the permission of the publisher, is forbidden and liable to prosecution. This applies in particular to reproductions, translations, microfilming, and storage and processing in electronic retrieval systems.

This publication has been peer reviewed.

www.peterlang.com

To Young University Graduates

Preface

Since a young age, I lived, received my education and worked in different countries. Afterwards, during over 30 years of work in The University of Gaziantep in Turkey as a lecturer, many students came to my office and expressed their uncertainty regarding what to do after graduation. Due to the fact that each student has his/her different personal circumstances and capabilities, I tried my best to guide each student to the optimum route that suits his/her personal conditions and field of interest. It is likely that the satisfaction of those students encouraged other students to do the same. In fact, the increase in the number of these events led to the idea of turning these advices and recommendations into a seminar. The seminar was presented twice several years ago and was welcomed by all students, after which even more students and graduates came to me for similar consultations.

The events explained in the previous paragraph inspired me to develop and expand the contents of the seminar into a concise book that should not be too detailed or boring to the reader, particularly for students who are usually less patient than matured ones. The idea of writing this book initiated several years ago when I found that there is a lack of such book in libraries which concentrates specifically on the sensitive stage of young students that are about to be graduated, and on those that are newly graduated. It is obvious that the contents of this book are directed equally to both genders; however, in order not to repeat the "he/she" term for the third person, I decided to use just "he" instead, and similarly, instead of "his/her", to use "his" only.

I observed that most new graduates have a happy feeling for being free from the stress of exams, and for being free from being financially dependent on their parents or other sources. However, this happy feeling is usually accompanied with various degrees of anxiety, and sometimes even fear, from the unknown future. This stress increases with the existence of several choices or alternative routes to follow after the graduation stage, and also, when the best or optimum alternative is unclear and/or uncertain regarding its durability in being the optimum choice. This uncertainty is usually due to several factors, such as the lack of life experience and to being extremely busy most of the time with undergraduate studies. Moreover, influence of some of these factors may appear to be variable with time and/or according to each region or country. These variations are usually related to the stability of the countries in relevance to the economy, politics, social security and other factors.

Most of the courses given in universities deliver reasonably sufficient knowledge about the subjects of the course in concern without indicating much to the influence of the human factor and human relations on the practical side of it, which is the work stage after graduation. During my long period of work as a lecturer, I frequently presented these sensitive matters in my lectures. The appreciation of the practical advices given to students during my lectures was not clear during the lecture delivery; however, it was clearly positive from the feed-back of the graduated ones after they started working.

The selection of the optimum route to follow after graduation requires good knowledge of the advantages and disadvantages of each available alternative route. The incomplete and/or uncertain knowledge in the mind of students and young graduates is what led me to allocate time and effort to write this book. Due to their being busy with their jobs/duties which are likely to be relevant to a different profession, many parents and family friends may not have that knowledge which is urgently needed for new graduates. Despite the fact that most lecturers are usually ready to guide students in such sensitive matter, students usually feel shy to seek their guidance simply due to different reasons, mainly due to thinking that the lecturers have no time to discuss the matter in detail. In fact, if a lecturer gives a quick reply and advice to students in general without learning the details of the circumstances of each specific student or a new graduate, the given advice may not be the optimum for that person. However, this may be discovered when it is too late to change it.

For someone to live in different countries for long periods may appear to others as a lucky thing, which is correct in some aspects, while in other aspects of life this is accompanied with some disadvantages. One of these disadvantages is the unpleasant feeling of being treated as a foreigner almost everywhere. The same feeling may continue even after returning back to own country. This could be due to having an accent and some other factors. For different personal reasons, I lived for long periods in different countries and this enabled me to gain a broad view of life, different cultures and work experience. With good intention, I aim to enlighten new graduates regarding how to be successful and avoid being trapped by some mean individuals or companies. Despite this book being written in Turkiye, it is necessary to emphasize that the precautions recommended within the text of this book regarding some different mean actions were observed in several countries and never restricted to the country where it is written.

One of the advantages of living abroad in different countries for long periods is to get the chance to learn different languages. Here, I thought to benefit from this advantage and write this book simultaneously in the three languages English, Turkish and Arabic, with the hope that these three versions would ease the contents being conveyed to readers in different countries. Despite that I am basically a civil engineer, I tried to arrange the contents of this book in a way to be useful for young graduates of different fields of science.

I feel just like being a father who is keen to explain to his grown up children the best way to succeed in life, avoid the common mistakes, and be aware of the tricks and mean actions that may be encountered. After reading the advices presented in this book, it is up to each reader to take them seriously or simply ignore them. Due to the contents of this book being derived fully from my observations and experience in life, I did not allocate a section for references at the end of it.

Mazen Kavvas
05 Augost, 2021

I wish to express my sincere thanks to my dear family for their encouragement and patience during writing this book. Also, endless appreciation and thanks are due to my dear colleague and friend Prof. Dr. İsmail Özsabuncuoğlu for his invaluable suggestions.

Contents

Chapter 1 Introduction 15

Chapter 2 During the B.Sc. 17

Chapter 3 After Graduation 23

Chapter 4 Choices After Graduation 29
    4.1. Work in Your Native Country 30
        4.1.1. Work in Government Sector 31
        4.1.2. Work as a Professional in the Army 31
        4.1.3. Work in a Private Sector 32
    4.2. Work Abroad 33
        4.2.1. The Advantages 33
        4.2.2. The Disadvantages 34
    4.3. Postgraduate Studies 37
        4.3.1. M.Sc. Degree 38
        4.3.2. Ph.D. Degree 40
        4.3.3. Studying at Home or Abroad 41
    4.4. Privately Owned Business 45
    4.5. Serve the Compulsory Army Service 45
    4.6. Work in a Different Profession 46

Chapter 5 The Interview 49

Chapter 6 The Contract 59

Chapter 7 At Work 67

7.1.	General Recommendations 67
7.2.	Being in an Administrative Position 82
7.3.	Signing Documents 87
7.4.	Working Abroad 89

Chapter 8 Conclusion 97

Chapter 1 Introduction

Despite the fact that most advanced scientific research and inventions that are kept secret for different reasons, the classic scientific knowledge is taught in schools and universities in order to save the time, money and effort needed to research and find what has been already found. Similarly in life and at work, if you forget an important event that harmed you in anyway, you may go through the same painful event once again sometime in the future. They say about painful events/experiences: to forget is to repeat. Since life is too short to experience everything personally, it is always recommended to be a good observer and learn not only from one's own mistakes, but also from observing the mistakes of others.

The contents of this book represent a combination of my observation during my professional life, feed-back of graduates, and also from observations conveyed to me by friends and colleagues at work in different countries. This is in addition to some personal experience. I think that it is essential to convey life experience to young ones (professional and otherwise) in order to ease their progress, minimize their mistakes and minimize the cases when they are taken advantage of. After all, life is too short to adventure personally in every field of life. If one does that, he will not have much time or money left to apply what has been learned, just like what the Chinese proverb says: "Experience is a comb given to us by nature when we are bald." This book represents an attempt to deliver a comb to the readers before losing their hair.

The determination of the relatively better choice requires a good knowledge of the advantages and disadvantages of each alternative route to be selected after graduation. In order to achieve this knowledge, I always recommend seeking advices from reliable and experienced wise persons before making the final decision in any aspect of personal and professional life. In fact, it is most recommended to consult more than one person of such properties regarding the same subject. The reason for this is simply because each adviser is likely to submit a different opinion/solution that is derived from his personal experience and according to his view of life in general. After consulting more than one reliable friend and professional about the same subject, one must always accept the responsibility of the consequences resulting from the final decision and not blame that who recommended the decision. In this book, the aim is simply to clarify the advantages and disadvantages of each choice regarding what is best to do after graduation, and also, to warn against the common mistakes/risks that may have negative consequences on the quality of both personal and professional life.

Unfortunately, there are times when anyone may encounter mean individuals and even mean companies that, in different ways, try to take advantage of young inexperienced graduates. Sometimes, it is observed that even matured professionals may be cheated due to being straight and honest and for not knowing the mean tricks and traps that others may be fully devoted to invent. Here, the matter of exposing these mean tricks at work becomes more needed to be presented explicitly, particularly when the law cannot do much about the matter due to different reasons. Unfortunately, it is commonly observed that most of those cheated individuals feel too proud to tell others about their painful ordeals. This is mainly due to their expectations that others (friends, colleagues and the like) may describe them as being naive for being cheated. Consequently, the traps and cheating events are likely to keep being unknown to most others, and consequently, this allows others to fall in the same trap yet again. Some of the common tricks/traps that graduates may encounter during their professional life are presented in this book with the hope that readers will have their eyes wide open against such encountered mean behavior. Moreover, they must avoid being shy or afraid when they feel that they are about to fall in a traps.

The recommendations and advices given in this book may need to be modified by the time due to the continuous changes in the circumstances of life in its all aspects everywhere in the world. Due to different reasons, these changes are observed more clearly during the recent decades. Moreover, work opportunities and conditions may significantly change by the time even within the different regions of the same country. Therefore, the reader is recommended to investigate and foresee the future in the country and region where he plans to work and settle.

Chapter 2   During the B.Sc.

I think that being intelligent means being capable of being excellent in all aspects of life and not only in a specific profession. Despite that there is little known about the social life of Leonardo Davinci, he is a good example of the intelligent person for being excellent in any field of science and art he worked on. I see that intelligence includes a broad variety of properties such as self-control, self-development whenever required, being simultaneously gentle and strong, being honest and fair, being sociable and even funny with reasonable degree according to the surrounding environment, helping those in need without the knowledge of others, being patient as long as necessary, and many other similar positive properties. Many individuals may be excellent in their profession but less than that in other fields of life. I think that the latter case may represent a good professional but not an intelligent person.

The previous paragraph aims to encourage students to make the best of their physical and mental capabilities in all aspects of life during and after their studies for the B.Sc. degree, and also, remember that whatever effort is given during that stage of life will be rewarded many times fold after graduation. The world is getting more crowded, and the race to get a decent job with decent salary is getting more difficult. Accordingly, the competition in that race requires serious work and concentration. Briefly, hard work and patience are the primary conditions for winning this race.

The following brief recommendations are directed to those that have not graduated yet and are still going through their undergraduate studies:

1- During the starting years of undergraduate study in all fields of science, the basic courses given aim to help for a better understanding of the courses given during the final years, which are directly relevant to the practical side of the profession in concern. In fact, the courses given during the final years are a combination of new information and the information obtained during the previous years. Therefore, despite some students may find some of the courses given during the starting years useless or boring, they are certainly useful and good for them. Remember that eventually these basic courses will be of much use during their final years of the study period. Accepting this fact at an early stage should help students in being patient and determined to absorb and understand more material during those basic courses.

2- If the lecturer does not explain the fields of application and need regarding the course he delivers, then, do not feel shy to ask him to explain that matter. Surely, he would be happy to do that as well as your class mates too.

3- Frequently, students may think that ready computer programs seem to replace the exhaustive effort needed to memorize important theory, understand the way systems work, and solve complicated problems manually. In fact, learning the principle and logic behind the way to approach any problem along with the range of the expected results are quite essential before using the ready program that saves time and effort. This is simply because despite the ready programs being fast and improved continuously, they still may have some weak points, or even being frozen at some stages which are likely to result in an error in the results which may be dangerous. If the error can be easily detected due to the abnormal difference between the expected results and the reasonable ones, then, one may turn to solve the problem manually. However, if the wrong results appear as something that looks like reasonable while not being correct, then, using these wrong results during applications can be seriously damaging and harmful. This rough estimation of the program user to the expected results from the computer program is the only savior in order to avoid a disaster, and this is why it is extremely important to learn the basic theory and manual practice of the problem before turning to the use of ready computer programs. It is good to remind the reader that no ready computer program guarantees the accuracy of the results and/or takes the responsibility of the harm/damages resulting from any wrong results that may come out of running the program. In fact, the feed-back from the program users regarding the encountered errors, the lack of clear error messages, the dead ends, the difficulties encountered during data-feed and operation represent the main source of information needed for the software company in order to improve the program and produce a better version. Briefly, whether the program is good or not, the full responsibility of using the program would be on the user himself.

4- After passing the final exam of a specific course, try to keep your lecture notes safe from being lost or thrown anyway. This is important simply because when you start working after graduation, you may need these notes again even though you may be expecting to work in a field that is different from the subject of that course. This is because your lecture notes will be your best savior to provide you with a quick review of the subject due to being familiar to you. You should remember that, after graduation, the idea of buying and reading a thick and detailed book in order to start learning a specific subject within a short time due to work needs is likely to be inefficient because you may get lost and/or bored from the first chapter for being too detailed. Therefore, in such case, try to review your lecture notes first and/or read an introductory book, and if you still feel you need further details, only then, search for a detailed reference book. Thick detailed books are usually useful as references for detailed design and not for basic learning. For basic learning about any subject that you know nothing or very little about it, it is better to start with a concise book.

5- Try to build up your personal library. Due to the high cost of books, it is recommended to purchase the basic books recommended by lecturers gradually. Your library is better being of a moderate size due to the probability of your need to move into different cities or countries for work purpose. Select the most famous text books and pay attention to the units used in it (English or metric). Remember that most book sellers are not expert regarding this matter and/or other matters. Most of them know only the price of the books and try to sell whatever they have on their shelves as soon as possible. Usually, they do not accept returned books for any reason. Therefore, a preliminary investigation through the internet about the latest edition and its units is always recommended.

6- Try to remember that the better performance you show during your study in the university, the higher chance you will have for finding a good job with better salary and position. After graduation, your transcript will be fixed and can never be changed just like your identity card.

7- In case the economic conditions of your native country does not look bright, and if you see most others hopeless because of that situation, do not let this affect you regarding your will and ambition to do well in your studies. Remember that such conditions may change into the better at any time, and that wherever you go in the world, employers look for a good and ambitious employee with bright CV and strong personality. Remember that the history of all countries is full of ups and downs.

8- Try to buy a good general handbook that is relevant to your profession. Such books exist for every profession. They may be relatively expensive but extremely useful during all the period of your professional life, simply because they usually have all subjects of the relevant profession presented in an excellent and concise way. Such handbooks would be extremely valuable when you need or wish to review your professional basic knowledge quickly in case being forgotten.

9- From the linguistic point of view, English language may not be classified as the best language in the world. However, it certainly became the most common language on earth with no expected changes in the near future. Therefore, it would be better to work on improving your proficiency in English. This should be applied in understanding, reading, speaking, and writing. These four categories are different regarding the techniques required for improving each of them. I see no need to buy the expensive books imported from the English speaking countries; and instead, the local famous publishers in your countries are likely to produce books with affordable price, and contain English sentences and paragraphs that are translated into the local language on the same page, which saves the reader the frequent need to go through a dictionary. It is good to remind the reader that learning a language is best performed through small and regular doses, and also, through continuous application in order not to be forgotten. Working on improving the language should not be dependent on one single method. In fact, following one single method is likely to be boring and less efficient when compared with a combination of using books, CD's, watching TV programs in English with no accent (i.e. scientific programs and/or news), chatting with some friends and the like. Remember that at any time you say I know enough about the language, or about anything else, it is the time when your knowledge starts to decline.

10- The same with the urgent need to have good knowledge of English language, no need to emphasize the absolute need to learn the use of the basics of computer programs, such as Word, Excel, along with the programs that are needed for your profession. From the economic point of view, it is observed that the optimum choice is to buy a computer with specifications of an average or a little above the average in relevance to what is available in the market at the time of purchase. In other words, the difference in the specifications between the middle level computer and best one is unlikely to worth the difference in the price. Of course, this is unless the user aims to use specific programs that require very high speed processor and/or large memory. Generally speaking, it takes only a few months to see what used to be the best computer being an ordinary one, and there seem to be no end to these changes.

11- Wherever you may be studying, do not be influenced by those who tell you negative things about the university and/or department, especially if they are students with unsuccessful past. Usually, those who tell you such things are just trying to relate their failure to the low quality of the lecturers and the like. The proof of their view being wrong is in seeing successful students in the same class who attended the same lectures and went through the same examinations.

12- During your study period, try to be close to those that are on the top of the list of success in your class. Always remember that success and failure, hard-work and laziness, decency and indecency are contagious behaviors. The matter is just like going in a crowded traffic, and if that traffic is generally slow, you find yourself forced to slow down just like others without feeling that, and vice versa. Always review the quality of your friends simply because you are likely to copy a lot of their behavior without feeling.

13- No matter how difficult it may feel like, try to write your own notes during the lecture. Do not rely on the notes of others no matter. Remember that taking notes from lectures is a personal matter, and defining the important and unimportant sections of the lectures notes are different according to each student.

14- Try not to develop negative feelings towards the subject of a course and/or the lecturer. Such feeling is likely to lead to difficulties in understanding and/or learning the course properly. Remember that as explained in Paragraph 1 in this Chapter, all courses are essential for your profession and not only those taken during the final years.

Moreover, remember that lecturers are individual human beings and not teaching machines with identical specifications produced by a factory. Remember that nobody is perfect, and also, that you are different even from your brothers and sisters despite that you all are genetically related to the same parents and grew up in the same environment. In fact, all lecturers try their best to deliver good lectures with all good intention towards students. Obviously, the method/quality of conveying the knowledge to students/others is an entirely different personal property and/or gift, and is independent from the level/quality of the knowledge of the lecturer. This is just like when you hear a funny joke that can easily be understood and memorized; however, when you wish to tell the same joke to others, if you change any sequence in the events or even slowdown in some sections, the same joke is unlikely to be funny. Particularly, in developing countries, only some universities reject the lecturers that are not good in delivering their lectures, and the only condition for being a lecturer is to have a high degree in the required scientific field. On the other hand, it is unfortunate that nearly everywhere in the world the results of the survey/questionnaire given to students, in order to evaluate the quality of the lecturer in different aspects, are rarely useful or objective. This is due to the fact that the majority of students frequently like the lecturer who gives little amount of material for studying, asks easy questions in the exams, and is generous in his marks; also, they dislike the lecturer that has the opposite of these properties. After all, most students in the world seem to aim to complete their studies as quickly and easily as possible. Despite this behavior being wrong, it is difficult to blame them due to the high cost of living, being away from their family; and also for being young and inexperienced in life, and not knowing the importance of learning properly before graduation.

Chapter 3　After Graduation

Every human being has endless embedded wonderful capabilities since birth; however, the environment and available circumstances frequently suppress many of these capabilities but continue to be ready for development at any time whenever possible. This is just like having solid and dry seeds that, with care and good environment, may turn into beautiful flowers and trees at any time. Whenever the conditions are right, you should discover those seeds in yourself and let them grow. As they say: "Better late than never." After all, very few have ideal circumstances in their life, and this matter of developing the embedded talents is always a challenge.

Since childhood and until after passing the teenage period which accompanies physical and psychological stressful stages, one is likely to innocently adapt endless habits from the family and the surrounding environment most of which are good habits while others are not. Particularly after graduation when the stresses of exams are over, young graduates should start to filter those bad habits that seldom anyone draws attention to them, particularly if they are common among the surrounding family friends. This is an essential process/stage and can be performed simply through observing all quality and successful persons everywhere. This process should include all aspects of life. It is much better to pay attention to this matter as early as possible before hearing criticism from others later on when such reminder may make you feel offended. Furthermore, such bad habits may negatively influence your social relations and even work without feeling. The most common among such bad habits are talking with heavy local accent, swearing, not being clean and/or well-dressed, not being tidy, smoking, heavy drinking, being clumsy, being arrogant/show off, being radical in own ideology whatever it may be.

The previous two paragraphs are meant to remind young graduates to refresh their personality and be ready for a practical life as a matured person.

The following are recommended for consideration after the graduation stage, which represents a victory after several years of work and patience during difficult circumstances:

1- It would be rewarding and relaxing if you can take a short holiday and enjoy your success in the B.Sc.

2- Prepare your CV in English and in your native language. This is vital in order to explain your capabilities to employers everywhere. You may find in the internet several examples of CV formats. Always paste a recent and formal photograph on your CV because the face indicates a lot to for experienced interviewers. Also, when submitted, always write at the end of your CV the date of submission next to your signature. It is unethical and even dangerous to exaggerate your capabilities simply because this is likely to be realized during the interview, and thus, you are likely to lose your chance in getting the job. In the latter case, despite that the subject that you exaggerated in your CV may not be needed or important to the company, but the matter of lying (exaggeration is a kind of lying) would be the main reason for rejecting you as a candidate.

3- If you have a hobby, it would be good to state it towards the end of your CV without exaggeration about your capabilities. It takes a couple of questions from the interviewer to know your real level of knowledge in that hobby. If exaggerated, you may lose your chance to work there because the matter of exaggerating is the sensitive and unacceptable thing. Having good hobbies is given more importance and likely to support your CV in developed countries rather than the developing ones.

4- Without wasting any time, apply to go through one of the English examinations that are internationally approved. Also, apply for the exams that are required as conditions for working in governmental sectors in your native country.

5- Before your departure from the city where you completed your study, try to pay your lecturers a short visit, or even just say good-bye without consuming their time.They would be happy to see you graduated and free of the stresses of examinations.

6- Select at least three of the lecturers that you think they like you. Ask their permission and readiness to support you in case you write their names in your CV as references when applying for a job. Make sure that they will remember your name when being asked for a reference, simply because most of the lecturers have hundreds of students and graduates, which make it really difficult to remember all names. A gentle solution to this problem may be in presenting them your photograph with your name written overleaf along with your thanks for their help.

7- Remember that employees everywhere in the world do not like receiving reference letter submitted by hand from the applicant due to the possibility of the signature below the text being forged by the applicant. Although this event rarely occurs, the employer usually tends to directly contact the references indicated in the CV and ask them to fill up their standard reference of the company. New graduates should not feel offended when their request for job application is rejected due to personally submitting a reference titled "To whom it may concern."

8- Determine to be honest and productive during your professional long life. This is to improve the quality of the lives of all people anywhere alike, and also, to try to fight what is wrong. If you do wrong things to others as revenge because others did the same to you, then, you are not any better than those bad ones. Always try to remember that when others see you honest and hardworking, they are likely to be inspired by your character and behavior, and vice versa.

9- Remember that the quality of your character and performance in your profession will eventually be directly or indirectly reflected on your reputation as a professional. Also, this will be reflected on the quality of lives of your personal life as well as on the lives of your loved ones.

10- If you have some bad habits like smoking, drinking and the like, despite being described by some as being social habits, they are most certainly unhealthy habits. Some addicted individuals may know that these are bad habits, but always find a good reason for not being able to stop them. Their main excuse is generally being extremely busy with their studies along with the accompanied stress of exams, and the like. After graduation, this is the best time and best chance to get rid of these unhealthy habits. If you are in any doubt of these habits being unhealthy, just click into the internet and see what the endless scientific articles say about them. After all, how can you tell your children in the future not to smoke or drink when they see you as a smoker and drinker? They will tell you that they wish to adventure in these things just like you did, and obviously, they will fall in the same trap as you did. All those who stopped such addiction feel sorry for not having done that much earlier.

Try to remember how frequently smokers and drinkers insist on you to drink and smoke like them. The main reason is unlikely that they want you to be happy, in fact, they would feel better when they see that all the people around them do the same even though being wrong or unhealthy behavior. The one with healthy eyes appears and feels like being odd when surrounded by blind ones. Also, remember that no smoker started from smoking a complete packet of cigarette, and no drinker started from drinking a whole bottle. All started from very little doses for fun and/or to socialize but were quickly trapped.

11- If the university you are graduated from is not so organized regarding arranging data base for the addresses of their graduates in the internet, then, it may be good to exchange addresses with your colleagues even with those that have ordinary relation with you. You never know, you may be of great help to them in the future through giving them very little advice or experience, and vice versa.

12- Gather your lecture notes. Collect what you lent to others or ask them to give you the original after taking a copy of yours. Classify your lecture notes. Write brief notes about each lecture regarding the recommended references, and also, about the sections in the courses that you think you need to study more and/or were not given by lecturers at all due to the lack of time. Writing these notes may sound needless just after graduation when your memory is still fresh and full of the recently completed courses. However, it is amazing how memory can fail you when you need to remember something. Always remember the Chinese old proverb: "The faintest ink is better than the best memory."

13- Try to tidy up the information in your computer. During your study period, the stress and hassle are likely to result in an untidy and even scattered data in your hard disk. However, when you are desperate in need for a file, you may not find it, and you are likely to find it only coincidently when you do not need it.

After graduation, try to classify your computer data, select meaningful and short names to your directories and file which indicate the contents of the directory/file along with the relevant date, and erase the files that are repeated in different locations. In order to shorten the names of your files and simultaneously keep them easily understandable, it may be good to eliminate the vowels within the words while keep at the ones at the start and end of the words, such as "Infrmtn," "Prgrm," and "Fdlty," in which the brain can easily fill up the missing vowels between consonants. However, remember that the date of initiating a directory will not be updated automatically by the computer when you update one or more files in it.

If you have files of different contents and related to different dates (frequently updated or not), it would be good to write the date of all your files in six numbers just before the name of the file such as "200924-Chapter 3." In such name, the first two numbers indicate the year, the following two numbers represent the month (September), and the last two numbers represent the day of that month. This format of naming files enables you to see your files automatically arranged in a sequence that is in accordance with the relevant date, which is most useful in finding whatever you need with minimum waste of time. Tiding up your computer data should be repeated from time to time throughout all your life, and not only after graduation.

Remember that you may find a job anytime and need to move in rush away from home to another city or country with a flash memory or hard disk that should contain a well-organized and tidy set of directories, files and data relevant to your undergraduate study.

14- Since nobody is perfect, and nobody will be so, try to make it a habit in reviewing your thoughts and behavior even if there are no comments from others about these matters. Do not wait for others to draw you attention about your misbehavior in any aspect of life. In fact, most of your friends would not dare to do that because you may feel offended. This habit is good to apply during all stages of life without exaggeration; otherwise, it will be accompanied with gradual loss in self-confidence.

15- Since childhood and until after passing the teenage period which accompanies physical and psychological stressful stages, one is likely to innocently adapt many habits from the family and the surrounding environment. Depending on these influencing factors, most of these habits are likely to be good while others are not. Particularly after graduation, when the stresses of exams are over, young graduates should start to filter those bad habits that seldom anyone draws your attention to them, particularly if they are common habits among the surrounding environment. This is an essential process/stage and can be performed simply through observing all quality and successful persons everywhere. This process should include all aspects of life. It is much better to pay attention to this matter as early as possible before hearing criticism from others later when such reminder may make you feel offended. Furthermore, such bad habits may negatively influence your social relations and even work without feeling. The most common among such bad habits are those explained within the second paragraph of this Chapter.

Chapter 4   Choices after Graduation

It is obvious that in all aspects of life, there is no perfect case or situation without any disadvantage. Even the medicines we take in order to recover from illness have side effects. When the side effect overrides the benefit, then, one should refer to an alternative medicine with less harmful side effects. This book aims to present the advantages and disadvantages regarding the commonly available choices in order to guide new graduates to select the optimum one.

The following is a list of the probable choices where only one can be selected after graduation:

1- Work in your native country:

   a- The Government sector

   b- The army

   c- Private sector

2- Work abroad:

   a- The advantages

   b- The disadvantages

3- Postgraduate studies:

   a- M.Sc. degree

   b- Ph.D. degree

   c- Studying at home or abroad

4- Privately owned business

5- Serve the compulsory army service

6- Work in a different profession

The details of each section of this list are explained as follows:

4.1. Work in Your Native Country

After graduation, the chance to be accepted for a job in your native country or abroad depends mainly on the quality of your CV, and also, on the personality and professional knowledge you show during the interview. Unfortunately, as observed in the entire world, and particularly in developing countries, some other factors may play a role with variable degrees depending on the interviewer and/or on some conditions that are relevant to the company and/or government. Among those factors are the ideology, religion, skin color, the region of the place of birth within the country, gender, political view (ideology) , the existence of a powerful relative or friend of the applicant, and other similar factors. Saying that the influence of such factors exists in all over the world at different degrees does never mean that it is acceptable to do that. On the contrary, in fact, the absence of the interference of such factors with work and life is an indication of the country's development level regardless of how rich and powerful the country may be.

One essential fact that should be taken seriously by new graduates is that the job will not come to them. In fact, new graduates need to spend time, effort, and sometimes even money in searching for as many job vacancies as possible. This search is best applied without any delay after graduation simply because the available vacancies are always limited and the chance to find a suitable one is decreasing due to the increase in population everywhere on earth. Here, if a company or a government sector promises you with a good job even after an interview, do not just sit and wait for the final confirmation which may take a long time; instead, work on applying for other job vacancies, simply because the expected positive confirmation may turn to be negative, or, you may never receive a reply at all. If any of such unpleasant events happen, you would lose a lot of precious time through meaningless waiting.

It is unfortunate that racism and nationalism seem to exist everywhere in the world in various degrees with no clear sign of ending this inhumane trend. In fact, due to the general economic recession all over the world, and also, due to the world being extremely crowded, particularly during the recent decades, racism and nationalism seem to be increasing everywhere. However, there is no doubt that there are wonderful people and evil ones everywhere in the world regardless of the gender, color, country of origin, and the like.

Briefly, the graduate that is searching for a job should not think much whether the employer is racist or not simply because this matter is never exposed. The job applicant must depend fully on his CV as well as on his professional knowledge and personality during the interview and hope for the best. After getting the job, and if given the duty and power to be an interviewer at a later time, it is obvious that behaving in an unbiased way throughout the interview would be the most honorable way to combat racism, otherwise, repeating what one used to complain about (as a kind of revenge) is the worst thing that can be done.

In relevance to the comparison between working in a government sector, including the army, and private sector, there are properties that can be generally observed with rare exceptions. The relevant main advantages and disadvantages may be presented briefly as follows:

4.1.1. Work in Government Sector

In government jobs, you certainly feel relatively safer regarding not having unpleasant surprises at work such as not getting your monthly salary or being suddenly fired without prior notice as sometimes observed in private sectors. Generally speaking, if you work hard in government-relevant sectors, your boss is likely to appreciate it simply because your success means indirectly his success despite that the direct financial rewards to the sector and/or on you may be little or nonexistent. However, on the long term, you may see rewards in being promoted and the like, which means a higher salary. In government, promotions are slow and the salaries are relatively less when compared with those of the private sector. However, it is really good to know that the salaries in government are given on a standard and fair basis without any need for bargaining as may be needed in private sectors. In some countries, it is observed that personal life, ideology and politics may interfere with the promotion matter.

4.1.2. Work as a Professional in the Army

The army in all countries of the world is usually the strongest government sector, and may be considered as one of the best alternative choices in many aspects. In the army, the financial support allocated for all activities is observed to be higher than that given to the civil governmental sectors.

This is in addition to the army being given the highest priority among all government sectors regardless of the economic condition of the relevant country. If you are fit and qualified to join the army as a professional or as a soldier, then, this choice certainly worth consideration. However, it may be good to remember that life in the army is different from that in the city. In all armies of the world, the total obedience to the orders of the commander/s is compulsory with no chance for discussion or dispute. This matter may not be acceptable to some individuals and should be well considered before taking that direction. One more thing to remember that is in the army nearly all officers must change the location of their work and service within the same country from time to time, and in some rare cases, move into another country.

4.1.3. Work in a Private Sector

Working in a private sector may be attractive, and even financially more rewarding when compared with the government sector. However, the best way to get a strong and stable position in a good company is to prove being excellent in your profession and being able to increase the profits of the company much more than the salary they pay you, which is the basic formula to keep you employed. Unfortunately, some private companies follow unfair and unethical ways in order to minimize their spending on the salary of their employees. In fact, wherever such devious mean methods seem to be commonly practiced in a specific company, this indicates that they do not care about their reputation for two possible reasons. The first reason is being strongly supported by the government to a limit that it does not care about the opinion of the employees, and the second is that it may be preparing to declare its bankruptcy. These devious methods will be explained in Chapters 6 and 7. It should be remembered that in private sector, the main purpose of the company is maximizing the profit. Here, it is normal that during the interview, there will be a kind of bargain regarding the salary of the job seeker. All private sectors try their best to employ highly qualified staff to work for them while paying them the minimum possible salary. Moreover, working in the main branch (or head quarter) or in main project bid winning company, is usually better and safer in many ways compared to working in remote branches of the company and/or with sub-contractor companies. In order to be more attractive in all aspects and gain more trust, all private companies try to exaggerate their capabilities and the number and size of their completed works/projects.

4.2. Work Abroad

In many cases, particularly when the economic conditions are not bright in the country of origin and/or graduation, the idea of working abroad may appear to be attractive due to different reasons. Some of the reasons for taking this decision are getting better salaries in foreign currencies, learning a lot from large projects, going through an interesting social adventure, and the like. These factors may be true in variable degrees depending on the quality of the company as well as on the targeted country. However, the applicant must be careful in selecting the country, where the job is promised, regarding several factors among which security, social stability and economic growth of the country. Again, these matters depend on the quality and reliability of the employer company as well as on other factors explained in Chapters 6 and 7.

4.2.1. The Advantages

The main advantages of working abroad may be presented briefly as follows:

a- Being in a different country widens your view about life and work in general, and also, increases you knowledge about different cultures. Eventually, you will see that all people in the world are the same regarding their thinking and expectations from life, and that there are good and bad individuals everywhere.

b- It increases the chance of getting in touch with professionals from different countries, which in turn, is likely to open other new opportunities for you after the completion of period of your contract, particularly if you learn the language of the host country and adopt to live in it.

c- It enables a better salary payment in foreign currency.

d- It enables for improving your knowledge about large projects. In foreign countries that give bids for projects to be completed by other countries, the projects in concern are usually large ones; otherwise, the mother country would do it.

e- Working abroad for a long time with no legal problems in your record during your stay may enable you for getting the citizenship of the host country. This may open new plans for you in many ways, particularly if you learn the language of the host country.

f- When your work for a big company in an important project is added into your CV, it is likely to increase your chance of finding yet another job without any time loss. This would be more likely to happen if the new project is of a similar type and in the same country.

4.2.2. The Disadvantages

One or more of the disadvantages that may be encountered abroad are the following:

a- Feeling as a foreigner in the host country is never an easy or pleasant feeling, particularly when dealing with uneducated people.

b- After signing your contract for work, if you are not certain of staying for a long time in the host country you may not feel keen to learn the language over there. This may happen particularly when that language is not internationally commonly used and/or if it is a difficult one. Not knowing the language is likely to make you lonely from the social point of view, and sometimes, you may even worry about being cheated or attacked with no easy way to defend yourself. An Arabic proverb says: "Learning the language of a people saves you from their harm." As a result of not knowing the language, you may need to stick to some friends that came with you from your native country, and this is unlikely to help you learn much about the language, culture, habits and/or style of life in the host country. In other words, your stay over there may be boring and tiring.

c- If your stay is long in the host country, and eventually you learn the basics of its language, you may find a friend of the other sex which, after a long friendship, may tend to consider the idea of marriage. This event happens frequently particularly when the x-candidate/s for marriage in your native country are out of sight for a long time. A proverb in both Arab countries and in Turkey says: "Whoever is out of sight will eventually be out of the heart." In fact, the short term of getting married to one from another country may be good and promising while, in some cases, on the long term things may not be as one would expect and/or hope. One of the reasons for the difficulties involved in such marriage is that your need to spend nearly all your holidays and money on frequent travel between the two countries. Moreover, after several years of marriage, it is common to see each of the couple insisting to stay in their motherland and not otherwise. If the husband and wife are of different religions and respect each another's religion and believes, after having children, a typical dispute is likely to arise about which religion the children should follow. Frequently, in such case, the parents of the husband and wife are likely to interfere and stimulate such disputes. Moreover, in some developing countries, the compulsory army service may be applied on the males that obtain the nationality after marriage, and even may be applied to the children when they grow up. I frequently observed these events in many developing and developed countries. From my observations I think that, on the long term, the probability of the success of such marriages is about 50 %. Finally it may be good to remind the reader that, from the genetics point of view, it has been long proven that marriage from different races and countries is likely to produce healthier and more beautiful children. Moreover, those children will certainly love both countries of their parents, and eventually, this should lead to a step forward to a more peaceful world. In this Paragraph, the advantages and disadvantages are difficult to be separated.

d- When you return back home after a long stay abroad, you are likely to feel like being a foreigner in your own country. This is because most of your friends and x-class mates had been settled in different locations at home or abroad, and communicating with them may not appear to be as exciting as it used to be in the past before your departure. Obviously, this may be due to their being busy with their work and family (if being married with children) as well as to different personal problem that they cannot explain on the phone. Moreover, due to staying abroad for a long time, you are likely to lose precious information about how to start and organize your own business in your country due to the changes in the business, environment, economy, and the like of other factors, even though you may own good amount of money during that period.

e- Some companies that earn the bid for a project in a foreign country abuse their employees in some mean ways, and they get the power to do that from the host country, particularly when being a developing one.

Applying to claim for your rights over there is likely to be extremely difficult. This is mainly due to the language barrier, and also, to the unknown complexity and/or expenses of the legal procedures involved in the claim (solicitor and the like).

f- If your stay abroad many years without any social relations, and your age progress to a limit that you feel you should not delay the marriage matter anymore, your choices for a partner at home may seem to be limited. In such case, being desperate not to lose more time, you may select the wrong partner due to the short period available to get to know each another. Consequently, the marriage may not last a long time with painful consequences to both sides, particularly when there are children. The causative of the problem here is likely to be that both sides do not suit each another, and not necessarily that one of them is bad or guilty.

g- In order to solve the social loneliness in the host country, there are always those groups that show their aims and activities to be social, humanitarian, environmentalist, religious, and the like. In fact, many of these groups have camouflaged different mean aims, and likely to be dangerous. They may help you to get out of your loneliness, and also in solving your accommodation and financial problems. They may even promise to help you in different ways even after returning home. Usually, they are professional in attracting young and ambitious foreigners, and later on, in using them for their own mean purposes such as spying, missionary activities and even terrorism. Many fall in this trap which may change their life altogether into a real nightmare. The problem is that those who are trapped are pressed, and even threatened, never to tell anyone about their activities, otherwise, the consequences are likely to be extremely dangerous. Having said that should never deter the reader from socializing in the host country. The only advice is to open your eyes and smell any devious or political aims from any group that tries to approach you in any way, and gently reject their friendship and offers.

The presented disadvantages of working abroad may seem be repellent to most young graduates. However, if one is careful and wise during his stay abroad, it may be enjoyable and improve the quality of your life. It is always recommended that you consult more than one about the idea of working abroad, particularly if you can find someone who worked in the same country you plan to go.

4.3. Postgraduate Studies

The idea to continue studying to obtain postgraduate degrees should be carefully considered regarding several aspects. The essential matter here is the financial support required for the study period. Some may be lucky to have financial support that is sufficient to allow them to concentrate on their postgraduate studies, and other may get a scholarship for such plan. However, some may work simultaneously while studying, which is likely to lead to a slow progress in the research to a limit that may risk the whole study plan. Some students confessed to me that they intended to apply and register for the postgraduate studies just in order to postpone their compulsory army service. Others confessed that the main reason is to enable them to get approval from the company where they work for frequent hourly leaves in order to attend courses and/or visit their supervisor, while the real reason is simply to be able to go away from their work for different purposes. Obviously, the postgraduate candidates that seem to be doing these mean actions lose their dignity and respect. However, most of these individuals do not seem to worry about that matter, particularly when the university fees are nearly negligible.

Generally, during the B.Sc. studies, the number of students is relatively large. Accordingly, the likelihood that there will be a personal conversation between a student and the lecturer is slim. However, the situation is different during postgraduate studies through which the student should discuss the research subject with his supervisor frequently, and likely that from time to time have some friendly conversation. At any time, if such friendly conversation occurs, it is recommended that the student should never start discussing his ideology or religion or political views with his supervisor. Even in case the lecturer/supervisor himself starts a conversation about such subjects, the student should be wise enough to gently cut the subject short and give neutral replies such as he has no time to think about these things due to being too busy with studies and/or for these matters being too confusing, uncertain and the like.

Science and research are noble targets, and going for postgraduate study may be divided into two essential sections, the first is to plan for obtaining the M.Sc. degree only, while the second is to complete the M.Sc. with the aim to go for the Ph.D. later on.

Observers see that due to the increase in population of all professionals in every field, employers seem to be getting choosier in selecting their employees. Here, it is obvious that the person with a M.Sc. degree would be preferred over the one without it. To the employer, despite that the subject of the thesis may not necessarily be relevant to the project or field of work in the company, obtaining the M.Sc. degree indicates extra capabilities of the job applicant in investigation, in being patient and in presenting a good thesis that is written according to the local standards. Therefore, new graduates are recommended to go for the M.Sc. studies if their personal circumstances are suitable for such plan. This is recommended to be performed before serving the army (if compulsory), and also, before getting married due to obvious reasons.

4.3.1. M.Sc. Degree

For some readers, it may be good to explain briefly what are the requirements and stages to be performed in order to obtain the M.Sc. degree. The start should be in applying to the university you think best for you in more than one way; then, if the application is accepted, the university will arrange an appointment for an interview (may be after going through a written examination). If all seem to be positive, you should go for two semesters during which the student must complete a certain number of courses, after which there will be two more semesters for research in a selected subject and for writing the thesis. There is also the possibility to get the M.Sc. degree without writing a thesis, where the thesis section is replaced by an increase in the number of courses taken. Generally, only those that completed their M.Sc. with a thesis can go for a Ph.D. degree.

If a student wishes to apply for a M.Sc. degree goes through the probable written examination and initial interview, then, a supervisor will be allocated for him. During the first meeting with the supervisor, it would be better for the candidate to express his field of interest by selecting the subject of the research, and not say that he is ready to research in any subject.

The selection of the major branch within his profession in which the subject of the M.Sc. is to be studied must be carefully done after consulting more than one professional. This is simply because the selected branch or field of study is likely to limit your job hunting to those companies/sectors that work in the same field, and this is something you cannot change later on.

A typical research for a M.Sc. degree should start with a good review to the general background of the relevant field. This should be followed by an investigation about the achievements obtained previously regarding the subject in concern. Then, theoretical and/or laboratory application, following an existing principle or theory, should be performed with the essential condition that the research is not a repetition of a previously performed and completed one. In other words, the M.Sc. research is either an application of an existing theory on a new set of data/conditions in order to observe and discuss the results, or, the application of more than one theory on the same data/conditions in order to compare and evaluate the differences in the obtained results regarding each set of data. The results should be presented with a discussion and conclusion. The formats of the thesis must be compatible with the standards recommended by the scientific institute of the university. After the completion of the thesis and after being approved by the supervisor, copies of the thesis will be posted to three or five jury to be reviewed. Afterwards, there will be an oral examination during which the candidate should present his thesis briefly as a seminar during an average period of 30 minutes. This is followed by comments on the presentation and some questions asked by the jury about the subject of the thesis, as well as other background-relevant matters. If the M.Sc. candidate works hard in his research, none of these stages should be difficult. After all, those who obtained their M.Sc. degrees are hardworking persons and not necessarily genius. The common period to be allocated to complete a M.Sc. research is two years with probability of limited extension defined by the relevant university.

After completing the M.Sc. studies, if the graduate plans to go for the Ph.D., then, there are some essential conditions, such as his M.Sc. thesis must have been completed with a thesis, and that the candidate has been a successful with other conditions that may vary depending on each university.

4.3.2. Ph.D. Degree

This is an advanced stage above the M.Sc. degree through which the candidate is expected to prove being determined to work hard and allocate reasonably long time for reading books and scientific articles, planning for the way to investigate and analyze the results of the research. Briefly, the Ph.D. research must represent a step forward in science that has not been done in the past. In most cases, due to the time allocated for research, the target of a new Ph.D. research may be starting from the point where a previous Ph.D. stopped, and then, continue forward to a new point/target that is more advanced.

In most universities, the stages required to complete the Ph.D. studies are somehow similar to those relevant to the M.Sc. degree but with a longer period through which a proposal for new methods and new theory with new results obtained through the research. As explained previously regarding the M.Sc., the only need for succeeding in a Ph.D. research is to be hardworking and patient. The common period allocated for completing a Ph.D. research is a minimum of three years with probability of limited extension.

At this stage, I wish to remind the reader that after obtaining a Ph.D. degree, the chances for finding a job in private companies is likely to be limited when compared to those who apply with just a M.Sc. degree. This is due to that most private companies do not wish to pay a high salary for a Ph.D. degree holder, and also, due to the expectation that such person may be needlessly overeducated and/or overconfident to a limit that he may be bossy at work. Most private companies just consult the professional Ph.D. degree holder (academics) whenever needed, and pay them for their consultancy, and that is it. After one obtains a Ph.D. degree, the best place for work is in a university, and this is what is meant by having limited choices at work. Still, being an academic in a university is a respected and enjoyable job despite the salaries being less than satisfactory in most countries.

In relevance to the postgraduate studies in social sciences, the research concentrates on a broad variety of subjects, such as economics, education, geography, history, law, linguistics, psychology, sociology, anthropology and communication studies. In fact, the definition of social sciences may be briefly expressed as the branch of science devoted to the study of societies and the relationships among individuals within those societies. Some of these branches have clear interrelation with other branches. The research for the M.Sc. and Ph.D. degrees include a thorough investigation about a specific subject by means of going through literature survey in libraries and recent scientific articles. Sometimes, some tools are implemented such as the use of statistics and questionnaires. The amount of effort and research required for the Ph.D. degree is significantly more than that for the M.Sc. degree. However, the research for both degrees is supposed to be new and not a repetition or a previous research, unless the approach of the investigation is different.

As explained previously, the work and effort for completing postgraduate research involves thorough investigation about the subject in concern as well as the various proposed applications. However, the reader should remember that an essential part of the work includes learning whatever is required for selecting the most efficient computer program to suit the targeted investigation and the way to use it. Also, it could be the selection of the most economic and efficient laboratory equipment along with learning the way to perform experiments on it. In the fields of social sciences, the way to approach the subject in concern is the essential key to establish good and fruitful results and thesis, such as searching for the relevant regions and libraries, arranging reasonable questionnaires and rationally commenting on the results, performing interviews with the persons that are relevant to the subject in concern and the like. Moreover, the final phase of the research is to learn the standards required for presenting all the investigation and work in a good thesis with contents that are arranged in good sequence and reasonable amount of details given to each chapter. Being ready to present the whole research work verbally in a seminar and/or during the final examination is yet another responsibility that requires learning different techniques.

4.3.3. Studying at Home or Abroad

In fact, from the economic and emotional point of view, studying in your country is much better, where you are familiar with everything such as the language, food, weather, being close to your family and friends, and many other advantages. Also, even if the location of the university is in a city far from your family, it would not be too expensive and/or time consuming to pay them frequent visits. If the university is in the same city where your family live, it would be even much better for saving endless time regarding whatever is required for the daily life.

If national universities are not well organized and/or equipped with good laboratories and qualified academic staff, then, it would be better to study in a foreign university of a respected rank. This solution would be even better if the language of the host country is English. Obviously, this requires financial support which only few can afford.

It is important to remember that some universities abroad require foreign applicants to go through some examinations before starting their postgraduate studies, just as a proof that their background knowledge obtained during the B.Sc. studies is good enough to go on for the M.Sc. and/or the Ph.D. degrees. On the other hand, it is equally important to investigate that the degree/s obtained from that university in foreign country would be accepted and/or valid in the native country.

Most of the advantages and disadvantages of studying abroad are similar to what is explained in Paragraphs 4.2.1. and 4.2.2.

It may be good to remind the reader that in some countries, the education given in some universities became too commercial on the cost of the quality of education. In other words, it goes like with little work and effort you get a university degree if you just pay the relatively high tuition fees. Applicants are recommended to carefully investigate the quality and ranking of their target university in any country they plan to go to.

Particularly in the English speaking countries, the academic staff is lucky enough not to need to learn a foreign language simply because they do not need it. This saves them endless time and effort. Consequently, they experience lack of knowledge of the problems and difficulties encountered during learning another language. Frequently, if a lecturer asks you a question about something, despite that you may understand the question and know the answer very well (during learning a foreign language, understanding is relatively the easiest) but you may mumble and cannot express your reply properly due to your weakness in that foreign language. In the latter case, the lecturer is likely to think that you do not know the answer or your knowledge about the subject is poor, which is an extremely frustrating situation (not very pleasant situation as expressed in the U.K.). Worse than that is when you do not know the critical difference between the words that may seem alike in their meaning.

Sometimes, if you innocently use the wrong word in a sentence, the meaning may change totally, and sometimes, this may result in misunderstanding, or worse than that, in the other side being offended. That offended person is unlikely to show his feelings (not very happy as expressed in the U.K.). Consequently, without knowing anything about the reason, you may lose his support and even friendship. What is worse is that you are likely to keep repeating the same mistake because no one corrects you. The listeners may think that the reason for your impolite sentence is your being uncivilized and/or rude rather than being a linguistic mistake in your expression. In order to minimize such probability, it is recommended to carefully observe the facial expressions of the other person/s during your talk, and if you see an expression of surprise and/or shock on their faces, then, this should indicate a linguistic problem and/or misunderstanding. In such case, you should immediately repeat expressing whatever you wish to say in another simplified way.

Such sensitive difference may exist in the words "tell to do something" and "ask to do something." In English language, the first expression indicates an order like expression, while the second indicate a gentle request. In ordinary dictionaries, such difference is rarely expressed. Another example in English may be in the words "must" and "should," where the first word indicates certain need, while the second one indicates being preferable.

Usually, when the other side feels that he understands what you want to say, he is unlikely to correct your linguistic mistake due to more than one reason, such as to avoid interrupting you, and/or not having time to correct your language, and/or due to worrying that you may feel offended. When you use words and/or expressions and/or even pronunciation in the wrong way for some period of time, the longer that period is, the more difficult it would be to make the change even after learning the correct way. This is because you are used to say it that way for a long time. Therefore, it is recommended that you should do your best to learn the grammar and pronunciation correctly at an early stage.

When your knowledge about the language of the host country is poor, and you feel the need to think a lot in order to arrange the sentence before saying it slowly with accent, the listener is likely to feel bored. The latter situation is likely to make you lonely until you speak fluently. One of the essential conditions for socializing and having a pleasant friendly chat is to perfect the language and be able to express your views fluently, and even to be funny. Being funny and cracking jokes in a foreign language cannot be achieved without good knowledge of that language and culture of that society. Again, in a specific language, the jokes that are funny due to some words having multiple meanings are unlikely to be funny when being translated.

Regardless of the period of stay in a foreign country, it is clearly observed that those who travel abroad for study and/or work purpose while being accompanied with their family (wife and children) learn the language of the host country much slower than single ones. This is due to their relations being limited to their families and friends that are usually of the same native country.

Some may complete their B.Sc. study in their native country where the education is totally given in their native language, during which one or few English language courses may be given. In such case, some graduates may get the best marks in those English courses, and be able to communicate well in English regarding the daily spoken subjects, and likely to be able to obtain an internationally acceptable certificate in English knowledge. However, after going abroad to an English speaking country, there is that risk of coming across a mountain of technical terms in English during the first year of postgraduate study. Briefly, in English language, the effort required for knowing the daily spoken language is entirely different from that effort required for knowing the endless terms used during the study of a specific scientific field. Again, this gap in knowledge is frequently unknown and unseen by the lecturers in the English speaking countries. If the candidate for postgraduate studies is in the latter condition, then, it is highly recommended to take a course in English where the concentration would be on learning the terminology of the targeted field of science before starting the classic courses of that field. If such course is not available, then, it would be good for the candidate to find a time for himself (few months or so) to learn the necessary common terms used for the targeted field, otherwise, the efficiency of the attended lectures is likely to be seriously low and cause various negative psychological consequences.

4.4. Privately Owned Business

It is wonderful to have your own private business where all decisions and profits or losses are related to you, and you do not get orders from a boss about what to do, particularly if you do not agree about the correctness of his opinion and administration. However, it is obvious that such plan requires significantly large capital to start with, particularly that the start is likely to be slow with the probability of delay in getting profits.

If the new graduate has such a plan for his future even with the availability of sufficient financial sources to start with, then, it would be much better to work in a company for some time in order to gain some experience before starting his own business. This is simply because having sufficient financial sources is not all what is needed for a business to succeed, and there are always many work-relevant procedures and steps to learn. Also, during such temporary stage, it would be useful to observe the main difficulties that the company may encounter and the best way to find a solution. Such stage of learning the way to run a private company may take years and depends on the type of business as well as on its size that is planned to start with. It is most certain that in order to succeed in such plan, there will be a certain need to have good links and relations with the sectors that are relevant to the targeted business.

4.5. Serve the Compulsory Army Service

After graduation, in case of finding a job seems to be uncertain or difficult, then, wherever required in some countries, joining the army to complete the obligatory army service may be a good idea to avoid wasting time by doing nothing. In fact, postponing army service several consecutive times until you cannot be postponed anymore, your physical form, psychology, work, family, and other conditions may not be suitable for you to go through that stage at that time.

There are advantages and disadvantages in completing the obligatory army service immediately after graduation. The main advantages are that the graduate is usually still young, fit, and likely to have no emotional relations (engaged or married) which may make it a difficult task in being away from family and/or his loved ones. Furthermore, during the service may give you a chance to get to know many friends that are likely to exchange opinions and ideas about what to do next after completing that service, and this could be useful particularly if you are lucky enough to get to know experienced professionals within the army campus. One more advantage is that both government and private sectors prefer job applicants to have completed their army service due to the simple reason that if they are recruited during the period of work in the sector, then, they are likely to leave a space in their work, which may disrupt the flow of work to variable degrees.

If the period of serving the army is long, as in some countries, the main disadvantage here for new graduates is that they may gradually forget the knowledge obtained during their B.Sc. studies. However, this problem may be turned easily into an advantage if, during the army service they are lucky enough to be given the duty of working within the army in the same field of their B.Sc. subject; also if they take with them a good handbook relevant to their field and review it whenever convenient. In fact, the latter solution is likely not only to improve any shaky knowledge about some subjects, but also give time/chance to learn some subjects that were not taught during the B.Sc. study due to the lack of time.

4.6. Work in a Different Profession

Although not frequently observed, there are some cases when graduates tend to work in fields other than that of their B.Sc. degree. This may be due to one of the following two reasons or both:

a- The graduate cannot find a job in the field of his B.Sc. This situation may arise due to financial pressures when the graduate is in desperate needs to find any job despite having no relation to the field of his B.Sc.

b- Due to different reasons, the graduate has to works in the family Business.

The reason for the second case (b) is that the parents of the graduate may have ongoing business in a field other than that of the B.Sc., and in desperate need for an assistance from a reliable person to increase the momentum of that business. In such case, no one would be better than their own son or daughter. In fact, some graduates may like this idea, particularly if the expected earning is higher than the given in other jobs even when relevant to the field of the B.Sc. However, some other graduates may not like this idea but have no choice due to the pressure imposed by the family and/or due to feeling of responsibility because the family spent a lot of money on his B.Sc. education, which is more or less like repaying his debt to the family.

In both cases a and b, the gained fresh professional information obtained from the university by the graduate is likely to evaporate quickly by the time, and consequently, the self confidence in the relevant field is likely to be decrease quickly to a limit that the graduate may feel shy and worried to work in that field after the elapse of a long time. If the period of such stage is too long, the obtained B.Sc. degree certificate can be used only as a symbolic decoration to indicate that he is an educated person with a university degree despite that it is not in use. The latter case is most useful for show off purpose when the graduate wishes to get married. The fact of spending several difficult years in order to obtain a B.Sc. degree without benefiting from it at all in the future is really pity, and can be considered as a pure waste of time, effort and money. Moreover, during his B.Sc. education, such person took another student's right of education of a university that accepts limited number of students. Obviously, in case family business goes bankrupt, then, the obtained B.Sc. degree is likely to be useless for finding a job, and this is due to the long gap in his CV.

Chapter 5   The Interview

Wherever and whenever applicable, interviewing job candidates is recommended in order to ensure positive results for both sides. This is simply because the CV of candidates gives only an indication about whether the applicant is in a position to be a candidate for the job, but not about the personality. Performing an interview with job applicants is the best way to check the correctness of the submitted CV and see if they exaggerated their qualifications, and also, to observe their quality of the personality.

In recent years, when the candidate is far from the owner (government or private sector offering a vacancy for a job), an interview through the internet seems to be a successful and convenient solution in order to eliminate the cost and burden of travel, particularly when the owner is in a different country.

The following are some recommendations for candidates to be considered before going through an interview:

1- Before going to the interview, it would be extremely useful to practice at home how to define yourself at the beginning of the interview, which is commonly asked at the start of each interview regardless of the profession. In fact, starting the conversation is, more or less, like starting the engine of a car; once it starts, it will go on with no problem. The peak of your stress of the candidate is usually concentrated just before starting the conversation, and afterwards, you are likely to relax more and feel relatively more comfortable. Despite that whatever you may say while defining yourself is already known to the interviewer from the submitted CV, the interviewer always wishes to hear you defining yourself verbally just to check the level of your confidence and fluency in speaking. Also, since this is an extremely simple question, it is usually intended to help you relax at the start of the interview because it is commonly observed that most candidates feel tense and under pressure during the interview.

2- Be available at least 15 minutes before the time of the appointment. Never go late, simply because this is likely to influence your image negatively, and even may be considered as a lack of respect to the system/company. In some cases, being late may even make you lose your chance for the interview and the job opportunity altogether.

3- Unless you have a beard, or, intentionally unshaven for few days (a recent fashion), it would be better for men to be shaven. You should be well dressed and this should indicate your respect to the system or company, and also, to your awareness of the importance of such event. Other than these reasons, being well-dressed makes you feel better and more confident.

4- Try not to have a heavy meal just before the interview as this may affect the quality of your thinking and behavior during the interview.

5- Some have the habit of filling the gaps between the spoken words and sentences with meaningless sounds or words, such as "aaaa" and/or "you know," and the like. It is good to minimize, or better eliminate saying them during your conversation. The frequency of using them increases with the increase of the stress, anxiety and/or feeling tired. Extremely rare friends would think to draw your attention to such unpleasant and deeply rooted habit, simply because they do not wish to break your heart and/or take the risk of you feeling offended. Many close friends and even your family may not notice the existence of this habit in you, probably because they themselves have it. Speaking must be clear and fluent with reasonable speed all the time and not only during the interview. Such habit is observed in all countries and languages with similar words used for each language. However, regarding this specific matter, the only common "filling" in all languages is in saying "aaaa." It is certain that that such habit is likely to go on all your life if you do not know and/or feel that you have it. Some other similar unpleasant habits are physical, such as frequently moving arms in a nervous way or rubbing your face/nose and the like. However, when being reminded about the habit, it would be relatively easy to stop it. The basic condition for recovery relies in the existence of that close friend who would dare to tell you about it.

6- During the interview, try to sit in a reasonable and natural position. Sitting on the edge of your seat indirectly indicates lack of confidence and tension. On the other hand, occupying all the chair with relaxed arms and stretching your legs indicates either lack of respect or being overconfident or an apathy regarding the interview/job, or all these factors combined. Do not fold your arms while sitting or standing. Do not forget that body language tells about the personality much more than what the conversation does. Experienced employers have good knowledge about body language and can read your face and feel your personality even without talking to you. Most body language relevant books agree that the correctness and sincerity of the information given verbally is evaluated by only 5 % while being 95 % allocated for from body language. This fact should not make you worry much. On the contrary, this should encourage you to behave as naturally as possible with minimum tension and stress.

7- The tone of your voice and the fluency of speech are always important during the interview as well as at work. Usually, loud voice indicates arrogance and/or aggressiveness, while low voice indicates shyness and/or lack of confidence. Something between is always preferable. Although rarely observed, when being under stress, some may even stutter and say scattered and/or incomplete sentences. The only way to minimize the occurrence of such unwanted verbal behavior is through improving your self-confidence and being calm during difficult times.

8- No matter how tense you may be during the interview, try not to avoid eye contact with the interviewer. Again, do not keep staring at him, or else, this may make him uncomfortable. Just try to behave and look normally. There are some who always avoid looking at the eyes of the other person. The latter behavior reflects clear lack of confidence.

9- During or after the interview, even if you are desperate to get the job, never say that explicitly to the interviewer. In fact, saying this will never change the decision about you getting the job or not. However, if you get the job, the owner is likely to behave as if they did you a favor and even remind you about that from time to time in a humiliating way, and may even squeeze your salary. The worse is when the owner asks you (or even order you) to do something unethical or even illegal in exchange for the favor of offering you the job.

10- You may be asked about the salary you expect from the owner/company. You should have in mind an idea in advance about what to say regarding such question without mumbling. In relevance to such question, if you declare abnormally high salary expectation, you are likely to be rejected immediately despite being highly qualified. In fact, you should expect any question of all kinds. After all, it is a test to your qualifications and personality alike. Sometimes, the interviewer may prepare some interesting/odd questions just to see your reaction. You should be calm and try to answer wisely without any exaggeration. An example of such odd questions: what is it that you do not like about yourself?

11- Try to behave naturally during the interview regarding the way you speak and answer questions. When you are asked question of any kind, if you know the answer, explain with medium level of time and stop. Before you stop, if you like, you may add saying that you can explain more if required. Usually the answer will be negative simply because the interviewer is likely to feel from your quick and clear answer that you know well about the subject. Never go on explaining endlessly and wait for the interviewer to stop you. The latter condition may be considered to come out of primitive behavior and/or as a kind of show off.

12- If the question you are asked is not that easy and requires thinking, do not feel shy to ask for a minute to think about it and then give the answer. This would be much better than giving an instantaneous answer which may be wrong. Here, it worth reminding that it is common in developing countries to consider the need to think about the answer of a question as an indication of weakness in the profession. The situation in developed countries is different where requesting to think for some time and then giving the answer is quite normal and may even be appreciated, especially when it is obvious that the question is a difficult one.

13- If you are asked a question about a subject that you either forgot or do not know at all, then, it would be wise to behave naturally and either say that you forgot the details of that subject or you simply do not know the answer. However, if you feel you can find an answer depending on your logic rather than the information stored in your mind, this may be a savior, simply because all solutions in all fields are derived and based on logic. In such case you may start in saying "I think ….." It is unwise to give any meaningless answer that comes up to your mind just to avoid saying "I don't know" or "I forgot that matter." After all, no one can remember everything all the time.

14- At the end of the interview, the interviewer is likely to say that he will inform you about the decision at a later time. In some rare cases, the decision may be explained directly after the interview. The difference between both is when there are many applicants and/or when the interviewer has to discuss the final decision with the boss.

15- When you reach the stage of signing the contract after a successful interview through which all details were agreed upon by both sides, if the interviewer or any representative of the company insists on changing anything different from what has been settled on previously, then, remember that this is a sign of the company being unreliable. The required change just before signing the contract may not be significantly important, but the action of postponing it to the last minute just before signing the contract is the mean behavior. In such case, never feel shy to just cancel the whole thing and leave regardless of the time, effort and money spent in order to reach that point. Leaving at an early stage such unreliable company is much better than signing the contract and get endless similar unpleasant surprises during your work period. Usually, companies behave like individuals, some can be trusted and others cannot, and rarely any of them change its behavior by the time.

16- If the candidate applies for several job vacancies, which is always recommended, some replies may come late. However, if a positive reply appears attractive to the applicant, in this case, it would be good to ask for an appointment to learn from the interviewer or the owner about some important matters that are relevant to the job. In fact, asking the company to clarify the conditions of the job and contract indicates to them that you are not naive and/or not desperate to get the job without any conditions. Even if the candidate is desperate to get the job, it is highly recommended get information about the following subjects before signing the contract:

  a- The expected salary.

  b- The period of the annual leave.

  c- The travel expenses during the annual leave (particularly if you work abroad).

- d- The expenses related to accommodation (in your country or abroad) and whether you should find it yourself or the company will do that. If the latter is the case, ask about the specifications (location, area, and the like).

- e- The daily working hours and the number of working days in a week.

- f- The amount of extra payment in case there is urgency to work extra hours, or work during the weekend.

- g- If there is an extra payment in case there is a need to travel for work-relevant needs.

- h- Health insurance.

- i- The location where you may be required to work (office or on site).

- j- The type of responsibility/responsibilities that you may take (should not to be outside your field of specialization).

- k- The period of the advance notice that the company should give you in case they wish to put you off the job for any reason. Also, in such case, whether they will give you compensations of any kind and/or ticket to go home, particularly if the job is abroad.

- l- The period that you should inform the company in advance in case you wish to leave the company, and in such case, about getting compensation for the previous work period.

- m- If the location of the job is abroad, ask whether the company administration will keep your passport with them or it will stay with you. The latter case is much better.

If you feel shy to ask, or ignore asking the company representative to clarify any of the previously explained factors, he is likely to ignore and/or cancel your rights in this regards. At any time, after you start working, if you complain about such loss in your rights, the answer is always such as you never raised such demand during the interview and/or during signing the contract. Governments are usually exempted from such behavior because these matters and conditions are always explicit and equal for all.

17- There is a high probability that when you ask for clarification about the previously explained important matters in paragraph 16, the interviewer, or someone else in the company, may say that you are different from all other employees in being so precise and doubtful about these matters, and that no one else in the past had asked such strange questions, and the like. Usually, the aim of such comments is just to embarrass you and push you to give up enquiring about these sensitive and important matters. The reality is likely to be that most job seekers ask the same questions and receive the same comments. This is very similar to the case when you go to a shop and complain about a defect regarding their product, and you receive the classic reply that you are the first costumer to complain about it. In fact, they know very well that you are not the first, and probably they know that their product is not good. Usually, they just try to embarrass you and make you feel as being abnormal. If you come cross such reply, you simply say that for everything there is a first time.

18- After the interview, and when you feel that you are likely to be accepted for the job, it is recommended that before signing the contract, it would much better to search for the existence of any acquaintances in the company you aim to work for. If that acquaintance (preferable more than one) is a reliable person, then, he should provide you with valuable information about all you need to know regarding work conditions and the like. In case you do not have any acquaintances in the company, then, at least ask some any reliable person (even from outside the company) to supply you with such vital information. Remember that it is not easy to change your job, and accordingly, you must be careful in making sure that you will get fair salary and treatment in exchange for your work.

19- If the interviewer asks you about your political or religious opinion, then, this is unlikely to be a good sign for the quality of the company. This is simply because the company is supposed to be interested only in finding hardworking and productive employees.

20- If the interviewer asks you whether you had applied to other companies and/or you had received replies, it would be good to say "yes" and/or "I am waiting for replies." If he asks you to tell him about the companies you apply to, you should gently refuse to answer this question, and do not worry whether the interviewer would like your answer or not, simply because he knows that such question should not be asked anyway. His purpose from such question may be just to see how fragile your personality is.

21- After the interview, if things seem promising but the final reply comes as negative, then, do not get angry with anyone in the company. Remember that selecting the candidate is their right and that in the future they may call you to work with them without being called for another interview. This is because all companies have data base for all applicants CV along with the comments of the interviewer. This data base is saved in the archives of the company just in case they need alternative employee/s instead of the one/s that had left, or, if the company wishes to expand their works and increase the number of staff. For this purpose, it would be better to leave with the company your mobile number and/or e-mail address that is unlikely to change in the future.

22- In all over the world, there are some unethical actions in which a sector/company may be in need for an employee but determined to select a specific person well before performing the interviews with the candidates. This may be due to that specific chosen person being the relative of the boss or being backed by an important person, or due to racism, and the like of different reasons. In such case, the announcement of a vacancy and performing all interviews is simply to show a face of democracy and equality, and more likely to be just to obey the rules regarding these classic formalities. Obviously, in such case, the interview would be a pure waste of time for both sides. In fact, there is no way to know in advance whether such a situation is going on regarding the advertisement of the announced vacancy. However, graduates must never worry or be depressed about such rare events, and just go on in their application with the hope that the interview is objective and that the company sincerely aims to select the best among the applicants. In fact, even when there is a specific person in the mind of the boss well before holding the interviews, if a stronger and more highly qualified applicant appears in the arena, then the boss is likely to change his mind and go for that better one. This is quite possible because if the general aim is to improving the system, then, the only way to do that is to selecting the best employees. In fact, due to complaints and legal claims against some companies/

sectors for being biased during selecting the job winner among several candidates, some developed countries legislated a law which imposes the installation of a camera during all interviews. This aim to use the recordings as evidence in case such disputes arise regarding racism, gender preference, and the like of unfair behaviors.

Chapter 6   The Contract

This chapter includes precautions recommended for consideration before signing the contract. However, as explained in earlier chapters, the presented precautions should not indicate that most private companies are mean and try to abuse their employees. On the contrary, only few companies would try to do so, which is a suicidal behavior from the business point of view. If the job candidate opens his eyes and is reasonably alert in all stages, then, there should be no problem or risks taken.

With or without the need for an interview, in case you receive the good news about being accepted for the job, then, before signing the contract, you must get clear information about each of some essential matters as explained later on in this chapter. If any of these matters is neglected and not explicitly written in the contract, it means that the company will have the right to benefit from these matters against the employee.

1- Well in advance before signing the contract, it would be wise to require a blank copy of the standard contract arranged by the company (if available). If the company refuses your request, this usually indicates that there are mean aims against you. In such case, you should simply ask them about the reason for not giving you a blank copy in order to read it carefully before putting your signature. The answer is usually unclear and meaningless. If they say that the confidentiality regulations of the company do not allow them to do that, and/or that the given blank copy may be abused. Your reply can be such as to ask them to cross all pages of the blank copy before they give it to you, and thus, there will be no way to abuse it. Again, the reply may to be negative. It is abnormal that you should sign the contract without having the time and right to read. If such event happens, then, the company is likely to be unreliable.

2- The situation explained in the previous paragraph can be remembered and felt easily when you start an account in a bank. They give you a group of paper (nearly a booklet) to sign on each paper independently without giving you any chance to read anything, and in most of the pages, there are some blanks to be filled up by you but they never give you any chance to fill them or even to know what the whole thing is about. If you try to ask them to get a copy of the given papers in order to read them before signing, you are likely to receive an unpleasant reply and/or at least an angry look. The same as in all private companies, they always say: we are a respected and trusted firm and you must trust us. In business, trust may be good in some rare cases; however, if one side must trust the other side fully while that other side has the right to suspect others and everything, then, this is unfair situation and even humiliating. Many famous companies and sectors fail in their business and go bankrupt, and history is full of such examples. Briefly, you have every right to read the contract in advance before signing in a calm atmosphere, and even have time to consult a solicitor if you like. Also, make sure that all blanks spaces in the contract are filled up by you before you sign the contract. Failing to do those important actions means that you are putting a target on your back, and in case of any dispute/disagreement, the court will not be able to help you. Remember that, in all countries of the world, the law does not protect naive persons and/or fools. Some devious companies approach the chosen candidate extremely gently and may even create fake friendship with him in advance before signing the contract. The aim of such behavior is simply to make the candidate feel shy to ask about any details in the contract and just sign it with his eyes closed.

3- Everywhere in the world, the law says that any agreement between two sides (or more) must be stated and signed by both sides on two identical copies to be kept separately later on by both sides, and never one single copy to be kept by one side only. This is simply because in case any disagreement occurs after any dispute, each side should be able to claim his right in the court through submitting the contract copy that he has. Any side that has no copy of the contract may not be able to claim for his rights in the court. The matter becomes even more dangerous if you leave unfilled blanks in the contract and sign it just like that. In the latter case, if you say to the court that these blanks were unfilled when you signed it, the court will reply in saying that this is your fault to leave the blanks empty without filling them. Consequently, the court cannot help you at all.

4- Respected companies usually offer a copy of the contract well before requesting the signature. In such case, it is recommended that the job candidate should carefully read all the details at home, and if all seem to be reasonably good, only then, it is safe to sign. However, it would be wise to consult an experienced and trusted solicitor about the sections in the contract that you cannot understand, or suspect, or detect some missing sections. Remember that, in most cases, the writing in small prints (sometimes written vertically on the side of the page) usually include the statements that contain the tricks arranged by the company in order to abuse the employee. Such statements are usually written in a complicated legal language that is difficult to be understood by ordinary citizens and can be understood only by solicitors. This practice is observed in all over the world. Despite the details of work conditions and payment may have been explained verbally to the candidate, if such details are not written clearly in the contract, then, the company may not keep its promises, and the candidate cannot legally claim any of those verbal promises. The solution is to insist on adding statements as an amendment to the contract, and this is legally accepted even if written by hand. However, it should be remembered that any handmade amendment made over the existing printed contract must be signed independently by both sides.

5- When the agreement is reached about all details relevant to the contract, you must make sure that they will give you either a second original copy of the contract, or a photocopy with the stamp of (True Copy) on it. Also, it must be dated, signed by the representative of the company and stamped by the seal of the same company.

6- Some mean companies may verbally promise a good salary during the interview. However, when they call you to sign the contract, you may be surprised to see a different lower salary written in it. The company representative is likely to say that the only purpose of doing this is just to reduce their tax bill given to the government, and they assure you that they will pay you the salary that was agreed upon previously. The job candidate must remember that this is a typical trick, and the company may give the salary that was agreed upon verbally for several months, and even more than that during which they give receipts that state only the amount of payment with a date but without any indication for being relevant to the salary of a specific month or year. When any disagreement arises, and usually there will be, and if things are directed to the court, the company will say that the money given to you is much more than the salary stated in the contract, and that it was only an advanced payment with good intension due to your urgent financial need and request of the employee. Usually, the result of such dispute is that you must pay back the company the difference between the salary that was written in the contract and whatever was given to you during the period of work. In such case, you certainly cannot do anything from the legal point of view simply because the court follows the details of the agreement written in the contract and nothing else. In fact, during all the period of your work if the company pays you the relatively higher salary which has been agreed upon verbally, such action would be illegal and not ethical due to practicing tax evasion.

7- When seeking a job, the biggest mistake you may make is to work without any written contract and just a verbal friendly agreement. Observations show that such job is likely to be short lived, and the employee is likely to get his salaries irregularly, or, with an amount that is less than promised, or simply get no salaries at all. This event frequently happens particularly when there is a high ratio of unemployment which opens the door for companies to abuse their employees this way. Obviously, in such case, if during your working period an accident happens to you, you cannot have a health insurance for treatment.

8- After signing a contract that seems reasonable, some companies just stop paying salaries for four or five months (for example) with the excuse that the expected payment from the government or from the main contractor has not been received yet, and ask the employees to be patient about the matter. After such period, the usual trick is to continue giving salaries (one by one) that are always four or five months late. This is likely to continue this way until the employee is fed up and wishes to leave work. In this case, the devious company knows very well that if the employee claims in the court for the four or five months through which he worked with no salaries given, the claim is likely to take a long time to be processed, and also, that fees of the solicitor may be considerably high. Obviously, the claim may not be won because most of the devious companies have their own solicitors who know how to postpone claims endlessly and find a way to go around the problem without letting the employee win his case.

Here, I wish to say that as in all professions, there are good and devious individuals, and the matter is never limited to solicitors. Due to the factors explained in the previous paragraph, such mean company knows in advance that the expenses of claiming in the court for the unpaid salaries of the recent months is likely to exceed the claimed money, and that the employee is likely to just give up his claim and try to forget about this painful event. This way, such mean company may employ many job seekers and terminate their employment in the same way without paying their salaries during the last several months. It is easy to imagine the huge amount of money gathered by the company owner/s through such devious plan when talking about hundreds or thousands of employees. Obviously, when such company reaches a stage when no one would think of working with it, then, it is time to declare its bankruptcy and start a new company with the same owner/s and staff (who benefited from that trap) but with a new name, and likely to be in a new different city (hit and run). When any employee sees that the salaries are paid several months late, such action is likely to indicate the start of the trick explained in this paragraph.

In the contract, it would much safer if you add some important conditions such as if the company decides to fire you for any reason, or, if you wish to resign for any reason, the event must not be a surprise to any side. In relevance to this matter, both sides must agree about a minimum period to inform each another before separation through giving a formally written notification about such action. This statement simply aims to minimize the harm caused to the company as well as to the employee after separation. In fact, it may be good to have whatever you are promised during the interview (as explained in Chapter 5 in Paragraph 16) written clearly in the contract. Not including one or any of these important conditions in the contract, may be used against you despite being promised verbally during the interview. For any reason after a dispute, if the matter turns to a legal claim in the court, you cannot claim anything that is not included in the contract, and verbal promises just vanish in the air.

Finally, the following is a short presentation of an interesting but real event that may be useful to the reader. Somewhere in the government sector of a developed country, there was a senior experienced, meticulous and fastidious control engineer. He used to check all works executed by the contract winner companies and force them to repeat the works that were not executed properly according to the required specifications. He never accepted bribes and never feared any pressure or threat. All contractor companies hated him for being so perfectionist, and for forcing them to repeat the execution of many completed works. One of the contractor companies thought of a devious way to get rid of him once and for all. That company approached him as they need him badly for his being honest and tedious at work, and offered him a contract that is mouthwatering. He believed them, and after a lot of thinking, he resigned from his job in the government and signed the contract with the subcontractor. Afterwards, the subcontractor company gave him just one month salary and fired him immediately. The reason for this payment is simply because in the contract they arranged stated that the contractor company must give him one month notice before telling him to leave the company. That was the shock of his life. Obviously, after retiring from the government job, he could not return back to it and he simply gave up work and just stayed at home. The comments about this event are left to the readers. This event is clearly a very dirty trick but everything regarding all actions is totally legal.

As explained previously, a statement relevant to any kind of agreement is always extremely important, even if both sides trust each another endlessly. To emphasize this matter even more, I wish to present an interesting event happened to a dear friend who started a very large and expensive project on his own.

That friend had very close friends who worked with him several decades before the start of the project. Most of those friends thought to support him and be partners even though with their relatively little amount of money (they were not as rich as him), which was for them all their life savings. He welcomed the offer. However, due to all group being very dear old friends no one thought to put the partnership and the amount of shares in writing. Unfortunately, towards the end of the project, he had a heart attack, and unfortunately, lost his life. That was a very sad and terrible shock to all his friends. Then, the problem started after the wife of the deceased inherited all his money and all immovables including the whole project. After this event, the project was put for sale, and the serious problem started when the dear friends claimed their shares but the wife of the deceased refused to accept these claims because nothing was put in writing. I am not sure what happened afterwards because such matter is personal and it is not ethical to ask about the events that followed. It is a fact that anyone may pass away at any time regardless of the age, reason and location. This real event is not the only one of its kind. It is presented as a typical example just to show the importance of putting all verbal agreements in writing at least to avoid any needless disputes and/or injustice.

The events explained in this chapter, and other chapters as well, are never the product of imagination; they all are real. Similar events are observed everywhere in the world, particularly in developing countries and mainly in relatively small companies.

Chapter 7 At Work

This chapter includes various recommendations to be followed at work in order to show the path for being successful, productive and pave the way to improve your knowledge and position. The recommendations are frequently accompanied with some precautions in order to avoid common problems, some of which may be serious. Most of this chapter is allocated to guide those who wish to work in their native country. However, many of the given recommendations may be useful for those who wish to work abroad as well.

There is a section for those who may be given administrative positions, followed by another one which contains recommendations specifically for those who wish to work abroad. In this chapter, some devious actions that may be encountered at work are explained. In relevance to the recommended precautions, nothing is exaggerated in the following text and all details were observed in different companies and different countries with different degrees of severity.

7.1. General Recommendations

Some of the following recommendations may seem to the reader like what one usually hears from his parents or lecturers. However, they are essential and eternally valid for application, and many of them are recommended for application not only at work but during the daily life in general.

1- Work hard, and always try to improve your knowledge and performance. Remember that in life, success and failure are exponential. In other words, any success at work or in other fields of life is likely to lead to a series of successes, and vice versa. Try hard not to fall in the negative side because it is getting more difficult to save yourself out of it.

2- Be reasonably kind and gentle towards your colleagues at work. During every day, you are likely to be with them at work for a period that is longer than the time you spend with your family at home.

3- Your appearance is always an important factor, not only during interview, but also during work time, particularly if you work in an office.

Having a good appearance, that is being clean, tidy and well dressed (not necessarily too fancy), improves your morale and self-confidence.

4- At the start of work, do not get close quickly to a work colleague. Also, later on and for any reason, if you decide to decrease the social relation with someone, do not do that suddenly, or else, you may be break his heart, and worse than that, you may be creating an enemy for no reason.

5- Do not agree or disagree on the complaints expressed by others about work conditions and/or administration, particularly during the period when you start your job. Sometimes, such complaints from others may not express their real opinion and are said just to make you talk, and then, whatever you say is likely to be conveyed to the boss, likely with some exaggeration.

6- Never feel down if someone (senior or otherwise) humiliates you. Feel confident and remember that the other side, by doing so, is either an aggressive/complex person and/or likely to have a mean aim behind such behavior. Certainly, in such case, you must defend yourself by all means without losing your temper.

7- On a periodic basis (once a year or so), try to obtain a certified statement from the company which explains that you are working for them and that they are happy about your performance. You never know when you will need it and/or if the company will give it to you this way after a dispute. If asked why, you simply give them any explanation you like.

8- Remember that, at work, there is a real competition for getting a better position and higher salary. If you do not improve your qualifications and performance, someone is likely to take your position and leave you behind, and even may lead to your being fired. After all, working hard and being more productive, initiative and creative are fruitful and positive properties.

9- At the start of work, if you see the majority of the employees unhappy, try to ask more than one (separately) about the reason. Even in case you receive your salary on time while most others seem to be are unhappy because they receive their salaries several months late; then, this should be interpreted as a dangerous behavior from side of the company administration/boss. This is likely to indicate that your turn is coming soon in receiving your salary several months late. Usually, this is a common mean policy that some companies follow before declaring their bankruptcy.

10- In small businesses and/or low quality sectors, the boss may try to persuade or even press you to do things or sign statements/documents that are immoral or even illegal. Such boss may encourage you to do such thing through either promising to promote you and/or increase your salary. If you reject to obey request/order, then, he is likely to threaten you through different methods and/or even to fire you. Frequently, despite the required action being immoral and/or illegal, the boss is likely to assure you that doing such thing is very normal and commonly practiced everywhere, which is not the real case. Obviously, rejecting his mean orders would be safer for you in every aspect regardless of any expected negative consequences that may come out of him. However, the final decision is always up to you, along with the consequences and responsibility. During their visit, several graduates told me about being exposed to such pressure by their boss. I recommended them to reject any wrong doing and neglect any financial enticements or threat. Of course, there are those graduates who did not come to inform me about going through similar experience.

11- Following the subject explained in the previous paragraph, due to any reason, if you agree even once to do an unethical or illegal action that is requested by the boss, the same boss is likely to ask you to do that again sometime later, or, do another different unethical or illegal action. In the second time or the following one/s, if you reject to do that action, the boss is likely to threaten you in declaring your previous wrong action/s to others and/or to the court unless you obey him all the time. Eventually, the matter turns to be purely blackmail.

12- Never lose your temper, and never insult anyone even if they insult you. Even if you are angry due to the other side neglecting your instructions, if you behave aggressively and/ or insult the other side, you would be the guilty one while the real guilty one turns to be the aggrieved.

13- Do not criticize the work and/or performance of someone else in front of others, especially in front of his team of lower ranking. If you do that, the humiliated person would lose his respect within his team, and also, lose his authority over them eternally.

14- Due to any reason, if your job requires that you work extremely hard to an abnormal degree for long periods, then, the common long term drawbacks are likely to be one or more of the following, unable to:

a- Improve your qualifications;

b- Search for a better job/opportunity;

c- Have a normal social life;

d- Properly search for your life partner;

e- Lose your health.

15- If one makes a mistake that is offensive and may harm you, and you think that this mistake was made after planning and not inadvertently, then, you have every right to terminate your relation with that person and even complain to the boss about the event. However, forgiving may be good only if you think that the other person has tendency to change his behavior, which is usually a rare case. Obviously, you should be extremely careful not to be harmed again by the same person. Forgiving a second devious action that comes from the same person may be described as being naive. Some get their courage to repeat their wrong doing to others from the expected forgiveness.

16- The current trend of work everywhere seems to be in more need for digital learning. You must be capable of updating your knowledge in this aspect, or else, you may find yourself behind and like being chained for the continuous need of others to help you. Obviously, not everyone is patient enough or obliged to help you.

17- During your free time, try to practice preparing a seminar related to a subject that is related to work and explains the common current problems with proposed solutions. Even if you are not required to prepare such a seminar, you try to propose it to the boss. You never know, the boss himself may ask you to do that one day, and you should be ready and confident to do that properly and on time. If you search in the internet for recommendations about how to prepare a good seminar, you will see endless references about this subject. However, the very basic conditions to prepare and perform a good seminar may be summarized as follows:

General Recommendations

a- The optimum time of a typical seminar should be between 20 and 30 minutes. Anything beyond that period may make the presentation boring.

b- After the presentation, allocate about 10–20 minutes for questions and discussion.

c- Use a minimum of size 20 fonts for your writing with good line spacing. Smaller fonts may not be easily read, particularly by the viewers in the rear seats.

d- The pages of your seminar are supposed to contain only the headlines and not all the details that you verbally explain.

e- Do not use fonts that are decorated to a limit that can hardly be read.

f- Do not exaggerate in the decoration of the presentation pages. Try to make everything simple and clear.

g- At the start of presentation, you should define yourself verbally, and show your name on the screen in the first page below the title of the seminar.

h- Minimize writing complicate formulas and/or too many details. Those details may be explained verbally and briefly if required during the presentation.

i- Do not just read from the screen without explanation. If you exaggerate in your direct reading, the presentation will certainly be boring and all attendees are likely to wonder why you do not simply print the contents of the seminar and give it to them to read during their spare time.

j- During the preparation of the presentation, if you had obtained some sections from different sources/references, then, it would be better to allocate a special page for them titled as "References" at the end of the seminar.

k- Try to rehearse presenting the seminar at home more than once while recording your voice during every rehearsal. Afterwards, observe the total time required for the presentation along with the time allocated for each section. Work on minimizing your hesitation, time gaps (being frozen like) or mumbling during the presentation. Make sure that the time allocated for any section does not consume time from the following one/s.

l- Try to add diagrams, figures and pictures with reasonable doses. Make sure that the details on the figures and graph axis can be read easily after being copied or scanned. If necessary, you should edit their size to be easily readable.

m- After the end of presenting the seminar, some may ask you to give them a copy of its file. In this case, you should not be surprised about that. If you have worries of the probability of others taking your seminar and claiming its preparation for them somewhere else, you should lock the file with a password in a way that can be viewed without the capability of being edited.

18. Some companies intend to employ some of their staff for a short period only in order to avoid promoting them and/or avoid being obliged to employ them permanently. One more reason is that after they complete a certain stage/period that may lead to an increase their rights for compensations after being retired and the like. Such companies press their employees indirectly in different ways to leave their job and resign, such as overloading them with abnormal working hours or changing their work locations, and the like.

19. In relevance to a new proposal from your side and/or criticism about how to solve work-relevant problems, the way you approach the presentation of the matter as well as selecting the person you wish to speak to, are extremely sensitive and influencing factors regarding the probability of receiving positive reaction.

20. Gather projects, plans, and references (books that are relevant to your field) of a wide range of subjects simply because you never know when you may need them even in the same place where you work. When the boss comes to test your knowledge about a certain subject, you cannot say that I need time to review that subject. He needs to see your level of knowledge that is currently stored in your brain and not after a couple of weeks. In a meeting, if it appears that someone else

knows about a specific but relevant subject more than yourself, you may lose a good opportunity in a newly proposed project.

21. As explained previously, in case you need to learn a subject that you do not know at all, or know little about it but nearly forgot all, always start from the most concise reference and/or concise book. Afterwards, gradually move towards the more detailed references; otherwise, you would be lost and/or get bored if you start from a thick detailed handbook.

22. Do not expect the boss to praise you for doing your job/duties in an excellent way. This applies in both private and government sectors. The reason is simply that the boss does not wish to be in a position when he is obliged to offer you something in return for your good achievement, such as an increase in your salary, improving your position, a leave, and the like. However, the boss will certainly appreciate your good performance but unlikely to declare his feeling to you. Sooner or later, his appreciation will be expressed by a promotion, increase in salary and the like.

23. Even in some respected companies, you may see an employee that may be described as a perfect idiot and does not fit or suit the quality the good company you work for. Moreover, such person may be allocated even in an important position. The explanation to this is that such person is likely to be employed just as a returned favor in exchange for an implicit condition for winning a contract, or, a similar favor made to the company by an outsider person or sector. Sometimes, such person may be a relative to the boss without telling anyone about such relation. Usually, such a person may keep a low profile and just try to appear like working. However, in other cases, such person may know his professional weakness and try to make up the difference by simply spying on others within the company and conveying information to the boss. Such persons are likely to have inferiority complex and may be dangerous.

24. In most sectors, there are some employees that are used to do whatever needed to strengthen their relation with the boss, with the hope that this relation would eventually improve their position. This may be performed simply by spying on other employees and conveying the results of their survey to the boss. Such spies are usually friendly,

sociable, and may have good sense of humor. Their typical method in spying is quite old but considered successful in most times, that is to complain about this and that (which is not really their opinion) and then, just let you talk. It is always safer to minimize talking about others and/or criticizing things at work. If you wish to convey your negative feelings and observations regarding work-relevant matters, then, it is best to say it directly to the boss, or, express the matter gently and openly during a meeting. When working abroad, such spies may try to detect your ideology and political views, and check whether you are against the host country and/or against the system in your native country. Obviously, such matters are sensitive and personal. Particularly in developing countries, you may be in deep trouble if your conversation is recorded or even if there are witnesses to what you had said.

25. Most people are loaded with work duties and stresses. Fun and jokes are refreshing and act like a cure to renew our energy. Being funny is always pleasant to the surrounding ones. However, such behavior requires extreme care in selecting the subject, the timing, the speed and sequence of telling the funny event. At work, do not joke in the wrong atmosphere or in the wrong time, and also, do not joke with the wrong person (many do not have developed sense of humor), or else, the consequences of the joke may be negative and even dangerous for the other side may think you are making fun of him or disrespect him. Moreover, if you crack jokes among several friends, then be extremely careful that the contents of the joke do not break the heart of one or more of these friends. This is simply because many jokes can be offensive in one way or another (relevant to a specific nation, region, gender, physical appearance and the like). If this happens, the one (or more) with broken heart is unlikely to show his being unhappy but will decrease his relation with you, and even may dislike you to variable degrees depending on his personality.

26. Although being gentle and funny is an indication of high level of civilization and intelligence, unfortunately, it is frequently observed that, especially in developing countries, the image of the gentle, humble and/or funny person may be misunderstood for being weak or even naive. Therefore, particularly at work in such countries, it is recommended to limit being extremely gentle and/or funny. The best remedy for such misunderstanding is to get to know the other person well quickly,

and then, behave accordingly. Knowing the other person quickly is possible to a variable limits depending on the intellectual capabilities and life experience of the observer. In fact, generally speaking, an early evaluation of the kind of person/s you are dealing with is one of the most important and difficult matters in life. This early evaluation regarding the level of intelligence, quality and fidelity of the other person indicates to you the limits/distance that you should arrange your friendship with him. Whenever all observations seem positive, a strong and long lasting relationship may be established. Those who can feel and see the quality of the other person quickly and correctly are usually capable of saving themselves a lot of trouble, and may be described as being gifted and lucky.

27. Time is the most precious thing particularly at work. Do not spend much time through friendly conversations about general life matters unless the subject is work-relevant.

28. After the end of your daily work, and when being relaxed at home, it would be good to search for one or more alternative jobs. If such investigation leads to finding a better job, it would not be ethical to leave your current job suddenly. In order to minimize the drawbacks of your disappearance from your current job, you should talk to the boss and inform him gently and clearly about your intentions in working somewhere else well before leaving the company. In other words, you should resign peacefully and leave good memory among your colleagues and boss. After all, you may not like the new job, and think to return back to the previous company. This may happen in life, just like when you see photos of a place that appear very nice, but when you go there, you may be surprised to see it far different in many aspects. Many say that private sector companies do everything in order to attract you, but once you are in, your value decreases fast. Moreover, they may fire you at any time they like without any prior notice. The latter act may be avoided if it is stated in the contract that they must give you a three month notice (for example) before you are fired. Remember that all companies have an experienced lawyer whose a main duty is to defend the company against any legal claim that may come from any of their employees, regardless whether the employee was right in his claim or not.

29. At work, do not chat with others about politics, religion and/or ideology. Remember that, generally speaking, it is nearly impossible

to change the opinion of others in any of these subjects, and that it would be a waste of time, particularly if such conversations are performed at work. Furthermore, after a hot conversation, you may turn someone into an enemy in case there is a serious difference in opinion. Observations show that you cannot change the ideology or believes of a person through conversations, and the only factor that is able to do that is time. Even if the other person feels convinced by the correctness of your ideas, he is likely not to explicitly show that feeling because of being too proud to admit his being wrong.

30. Do not gossip about others. This is really a bad habit, and in fact, whatever you may say about someone may be conveyed to that specific person after adding some exaggeration. Gossiping is an unpleasant behavior and habit, and is a deeply rooted behavior in those that have weak personality. Remember that if one gossips with you about others, he is likely to tell others about you in the same way.

31. At work, after the occurrence of a problem of any kind, you may be given the duty of investigating and reporting about that problem. In such case, try not to think such as: is the reason this or that? This is because, usually, it is both reasons with different ratios of influence. It always good to remember that rarely there is one single causative to the occurrence an event/problem, and frequently is likely to be even several reasons/factors with different degrees of influence. Throughout your investigation, it is recommended that you should start in writing the probable reasons for the occurrence of problem, classify their priority order, and then, try to determine the ratios of their influence on the event/problem. This is essential to be applied in all aspects of life and not only at work.

32. Whenever being in any position at work, and even during your daily life, someone may ask you a favor (big or small), and consequently, you do your best to help with good intention. The same person may ask you the same favor again later on, and you may help again, and so on. However, sometimes, if this event repeats itself frequently, the favor you may be doing to that person is likely to eventually become the right of that person. Later on at any time, if and when you reject doing that favor for any reason, there is the probability that he may be upset and may even turn to be your enemy. An old Arabic proverb says: "The one in desperate need for something is harebrained." Of

course, this event does not always happen this way, and there are those who appreciate the reason for not receiving the repeated favor.

33. Try to observe everything at work. However, if you see a physical or administrative weakness/mistake, you must make sure that your observation is correct and not due to your lack of knowledge or understanding. Also, try to draw attention to the matter and/or criticize it gently and not in an aggressive and/or humiliating way, such as saying that things are okay but may get better if so and so is performed that way, and the like. If you say openly that the current situation is bad and a waste of money and time, you would be creating, needlessly, new enemies, and moreover, you are likely to break the hearts of several persons. Without your knowledge, those that caused the wrong doing could involve your dear friends (directly or indirectly).

34. Due to the lack of sufficient time and laboratories, the university education is unlikely to teach you everything in details. Therefore, it is extremely important to work hard on learning all the details relevant to the subject of your work. Learning the application and practical side of anything is relatively easier than the theory that you already learned during your university study. If necessary, ask others, and particularly your senior colleagues about anything that you need to learn more. Remember the Chinese proverb that says: "He who asks is a fool for five minutes, but he who does not ask remains a fool forever."

35. Even if your colleagues are used to perform their duties without any comments or thinking about how to make things better, whenever you see a way to improve the procedures and/or efficiency at work, try in more than one way to check that your proposed new idea/method is correct. Afterwards, try to propose it preferably during a meeting rather than conveying it to the boss through a private conversation. In relevance to your proposal, do not feel surprised and/or offended if you see opposition by one or more of your colleagues. Remember that most new ideas were severely opposed at the beginning, such as our earth being a globe, the internet, the mobile/cell phone, the fuzzy logic, and endless other examples in history.

36. Particularly in developing countries, due to different reasons, working as a team seems to be uncommon and difficult to apply. Wherever you

live and work, it would be good to try to encourage your colleagues to work with you as a team with the aim of improving the quality of work. If you cannot do that, then, at least you would not feel sorry in the future for not trying to do that. Moreover, do not give up, and try to do that from time to time. You never know, one day you may succeed in your attempt.

37. Be precise in the timing of attending meetings. Even though the boss may not comment on those may come late and/or express his being unhappy about that delay, it should be remembered that joining the meeting later than the defined starting time indicates lack of respect and civilization as well as not taking the meeting seriously.

38. During your work period, try to help other colleagues in every way and be gentle with them. This behavior would be appreciated by all and increase their trust and respect to you. After all, this behavior is what you wish to see from others when you are in need.

39. The importance of safety at work is increasing during the recent decades due to the positive improvement in human rights at work. You must know all what is needed about it and apply it fully. Any accident that may occur due to neglecting safety conditions may change all your life into a nightmare due to the serious legal and financial consequences, and also, due to your feeling guilty forever about the deteriorating (due to disability) or loss of someone's life as well as for his unlucky family.

40. The web sites of most companies are seldom updated due to the matter being time consuming and expensive. Moreover, web sites explain only the bright side of the company at the time when it was really bright and not during the recession period that may follow without your knowledge. Sometimes, the projects and achievements explained in the web sites are exaggerated. Even new and small companies show themselves as huge and wonderful in their web sites. It is recommended to read web sites without being impressed instantly. When you are in the company, things may appear different from what is shown in the web site.

41. If and when you are given the responsibility of purchasing certain item/s that is needed for work, you should go with at least someone else as a witness for all the procedures and conversations. If you are

alone in such duty, someone in the company may gossip in saying that you received bribes in exchange for purchasing the required materials. Obviously, there are classic methods in order to prevent such uncertainties that is in defining the specifications of the required materials, and then, selecting the lowest offer. It is good to remember that all shops and companies wish to sell whatever they have/produce and describe their products as being the best in the market. However, you need to be selective on a realistic basis from all aspects that are relevant to the product you need (financial, technical and the like). Sometimes the trick is hidden in the availability and/or the high cost of spare parts and not in the price of the set itself. A typical and simple example of this is computer printers, where the cost of the toner cartridge is nearly the same as the cost of the printer itself, and also the volume of the cartridge is clearly decreasing with each new model. The more you know about the specification of the required product and the available models in the market, the more salesmen will respect you and tell you the truth about their products.

42. Do not be attracted and/or impressed quickly by the appearance of new products in the market. New products, no matter how wonderful they may seem to be, may have some unknown and/or hidden disadvantages/defects that are likely to show up sometime later. Even if the producer sincerely believes that his product is wonderful, the efficiency and durability of the new product can be proved only through time which has not been tested yet. Such examples exist everywhere and all the time.

43. At work, there are times when you may be offered a bribe of different types and levels (money, presents, holidays, and the like) by different individuals or sector representatives in order to make you do favorable things for them. Besides the requested action being illegal and/or unethical and must be rejected instantly, accepting the bribe may be a suicidal action simply because the bribe offering person/sector is likely to arrange a way to prove that you received it, and thus, destroy you professionally as well as socially. Later on, the same side, without offering any bribe, is likely to blackmail you for taking that bribe in the past in order to push you to do further illegal actions which may be worse than the previous one. Naturally, the decent and long term good decision is to gently refuse any bribe of any level.

44. After your refusal to an offered bribe, sometimes, the same person or sector may tend to directly or indirectly threaten you. In such case, you must be calm, brave, and stick to your decent principles. Defend yourself in the way you think appropriate even if you need to convey the problem to the boss or to the police. Always remember that if you accept a bribe, you would lose your self-respect and self-confidence, and encourage the continuation of such wrong doing, which you may have complained about previously. If you accept a bribe even once, you are likely to go on this way (like being addicted). Inside you, your conscious will torture you all your life. Your smile or happy appearance will always be artificial throughout all your life. In such situation, think about what you would feel when you advise your younger brothers, sisters, and children to be honest and decent.

45. At work, and particularly after the elapse of a long time, you may have strong relationship and friendship with some of your colleagues. These dear friends are just like gold. Do not lose them due to any reason, particularly during some hot conversations that may break their heart and/or offend them. Remember that it takes several years to establish a strong and sincere friendship, while it takes just one second to lose it forever.

46. At work as well as in life, try to be gentle and patient in you treatment with those of low ranking and poor conditions regardless of the mistakes they may make. If their mistake is severe, just report it but never humiliate them and/or treat them roughly. Usually, their life and circumstances are full of problems that are unknown and difficult for others to imagine. They are in continuous need for respect more than money. Try to remember that this group is likely to be unlucky for not having the chance to live in a reasonable and healthy environment and/or get access to good education. Had they given the chance for good life and education standards, they probably could have become more successful and productive than those of the higher ranking ones in the same company where you work.

47. Do not talk too much, or else the value of your talk will decrease along with the number of those that wish to listen to you. Moreover, when you talk much, you are unlikely to be able to filter all what you say, and thus, you are likely to make more mistakes that may break the heart of others and/or put you in trouble. Remember that once you say something that you should not say, there is no way to erase it.

48. When being at work, and generally during your daily life, if you see your friend accompanied by someone else, try not to explicitly guess the relation between the two through saying: "Is she your mother?" or, "Is he your father?". Sometimes, saying such guesses may be extremely embarrassing to you as well as heart breaking to both your friend as well and to the accompanied person due to your wrong guess. The lady you referred to may be his wife and not his mother, and your guess that the man being her father could be her husband, and the like of such unpleasant situations. In such case, do not try to guess the relation, and simply ask your friend to introduce the accompanied person to you and let your friend define any probable relation, which could be just a friend.

49. During conversation, some may have this unpleasant habit of praising themselves through describing how they are decent, productive, hardworking, and so on. It may be okay to say very little about such matters but saying nothing is always better. This is simply because others should make their opinion about your quality and not to learn that from you. Such conversation is likely to be really boring. Try to observe this habit in others, and then, eliminate it in yourself if you find that you are doing the same.

50. Unless being too close to the person, and also, unless the matter is important, do not ask question that are too personal. Particularly in developing countries, it is common to do exactly the opposite. The most common question everywhere is to be asked even by anyone in the street that you never met before: where are you from? This question is common even if you are a native person, and nearly everyone seems to be curious about the region of your origin within the country. Some other common questions of a heavier degree may be asked by persons that may not be too close to you, such as: "What is your salary"; "Where did you find money to buy that car/house?"; "Why don't you renew your car?"; "Why don't you get married?"; "Why did you divorce him/her?"; "Why you don't have children?"; "Why you don't think to have more children?" and the like. When asked such unpleasant and private questions, it is really difficult to be calm despite that you have to be so and just try to avoid answering the question through changing the subject. Being calm is essential simply because such questions are commonly asked innocently with no offensive intention, and because those who asked them are uncivilized.

With few exceptions, the common reason for asking such questions is curiosity accompanied with implicit indication that they dare to ask you such question because they feel close to you, care about you and your problems.

51. Try not to hate one too much, and also, not to be too close and/or love one too much. This is simply because time may prove that you were wrong in your opinion and feelings. In that case, being extreme in showing your emotions may make it difficult, or even impossible, to reverse the direction of your relations. Such events are never limited to just losing someone that could have been a good friend, or, to have given your support, trust and sacrifice to someone that does not deserve any of that, it is mostly feeling guilty for having the wrong image about others and losing precious time and effort of your life.

7.2. Being in an Administrative Position

Dealing with human being and administrating others is one of the most difficult tasks in life. It is not only difficult to satisfy everybody, in fact, it is impossible to achieve such target. This fact should be taken into account before starting any administrative position. Even all profits were opposed by many enemies despite their aims being merely to improve the quality of life and establish a peaceful and just world. During your administrative work, even if you are perfectly ethical and fair with all others, you still may have those that hate you just for being jealous of your position and/or for your being from another race or region and the like. In fact, dealing with computers and machines may be much easier than working in an administrative position. In fact, an administrative position is likely to be appealing to most people due to the power and authority of the status as well as to the accompanied relatively high salary. However, besides those attractive advantages there are disadvantages that are frequently unknown to the person who is about to take such position. Briefly, the main disadvantages are taking big responsibility for anything that may go wrong at work as well as, in some cases, being put under pressure from the big boss to do things you do not agree about. However, since someone has to do this administrative job, when properly done, it should be appreciated and rewarded for being accompanied with difficulties that are rarely known to others. The following are some recommendation for those who take the responsibility of leading an administrative job:

1- Sometimes, when being in a relatively lower position for being a new graduate and single, you may be heavily overloaded by your boss to a limit that may make you hate your job. This situation is even more frustrating when you have to do things that your boss has to do. This unpleasant situation may last several years after which you are likely to be promoted to a level that is more or less like that of your predecessor/boss. At that stage, the thought of behaving just like your merciless predecessor may come up due to the painful years you went through because of him. In this regard, sometimes, the new position holder may do even worse than his predecessor. This event is commonly observed in families, where one or both parents were exposed to various types of pressure during their youth, and be rough with their children. Sometimes, observed even in politics where some individuals give themselves the right to revenge from the entire world after being exposed to suffering and harsh treatment for a long time. It is simply a human reaction/complex which must be prevented through self-control. Here, the problem is that the revenge is taken from the wrong innocent ones and not from the cruel predecessor, and such random revenge is likely to produce yet a new wave of complex individuals, and so it goes. In fact, if you behave like your cruel predecessor, then, you are not any better than him. Somehow, this endless painful circle must be broken, and after you get the power and authority through administration, you will get the chance to do that honorable thing in preventing the continuation of this harmful behavior. Looking down to new graduates and/or overloading them with duties are likely to decrease their enthusiasm to learn and/or to love their profession. Administration is an art. In order to be a good artist in that field, you must show ethical leadership, be fair, gentle and respectful to all employees. The latter properties will certainly improve the morals of all employees, help them to love their job and be more productive.

2- If you are given the duty of being an employer in a system that, for any reason, is in need for more personnel and/or workers from outside the country where you work, it would be wise to select candidates from different countries with equal numbers. This is because selecting a majority from a specific country is likely to result in that chosen majority feeling more powerful, dominant over the other minorities from the other countries. Consequently, this is likely to generate serious social and even work-related problems within the company as well as after the working hours. If applicable, the same principle should be applied even in the same country as much as practically possible while selecting employees from different regions of the country.

3- It is good to remember that good administration should not make everything bound to the administrator/leader; otherwise, he is likely to be too busy with many unimportant matters with no time left neither to solve the relatively important problems, nor to improve the progress of the system, nor to improve his knowledge about work-relevant matters. It is better to allocate a section of your work load to one or more trustworthy assistants while observing the way they apply your requests.

4- Although verbal deals are not recommended, when making such deals and/or agreements (money-relevant or otherwise), try to be accompanied with a dear and faithful friend. Sometimes, in case of any disagreement in the future regarding the deal, that friend would be your only legal witness that saves you out of that problem. However, it is obvious that important deals are supposed to be written as statements/contracts and not just be verbal promises. Despite this fact, some still feel shy to ask for written agreements, particularly if the two sides (or more) are friends.

5- Meetings are of essential importance for all sectors alike. Holding meetings is the best way to listen to complaints, exchange opinions about how to improve work, and solve the observed problems. Neglecting the performance of such meetings indicates weakness or apathy in the administration of the company. Such weakness is a negative sign of the company being unsuccessful which should be taken into consideration at an early stage of work.

6- It is possible to detect at an early stage some indications about the deterioration of the quality of a company and/or being close to declaring bankruptcy. Some of these indications may be ignoring the basic needs of the employees, such as quality food, hygienic conditions, transportation, paying salaries irregularly, and the like.

These observations lead to certain deterioration in the production; and moreover, lead to the employees lose their respect and trust in the administration.

7- Although their wages may be much lower than employing local workers, employing illegal smuggled foreign workers may cause serious headache to the company. This matter is particularly dangerous when crimes of different levels are committed by those foreign workers who know that the company cannot claim for anything against them in the court for employing them illegally. Sometimes these illegal workers may decide to go on strike and disturb the progress of work. Frequently, they may blackmail the company and press it to do whatever they wish; otherwise, they would inform the legal authorities about them being employed illegally. Briefly, the expected financial savings made through employing low waged illegal employees may turn to be more expensive and disturbing than anticipated.

8- In every stage at work, there must be at least one person that is capable of replacing another person after an unprecedented work leave due to accident, illness, sudden resignation after a dispute, and the like. The space left after such disappearance is likely to disrupt work progress. Moreover, if the person who left work for any reason knows that no one can replace him, then, he may consider blackmailing the company by threatening to leave suddenly and permanently. In the latter case, there will be no time to train a person quickly enough to fill that space. In fact, if you know a lot about something that no one else knows, it is unethical to blackmail your company, and you must convey your knowledge to at least one person or more in order to keep work going without interruption. You never know, you may need a leave work urgently for any reason and having no alternative person to replace you at work may make things really difficult for you as well as for the company. However, a company/system with good administration would surely consider such probability and is likely to do whatever necessary to avoid its occurrence.

9- At work as well as in life generally, it is essential to purchase and sell goods with the support of a contract/agreement. Verbal promises frequently go in the air and have no legal value. Many graduates explained to me having serious problems due to being shy to put the verbal agreement in writing.

10- In case you wish to take photographs during the different stages of your project, you need to select a suitable location where the sun light will be behind you and the view would be informative even after the end of the project. It would be better to take daily photographs from that same spot and even at the same time of the day in order to have similar shadows. In order to prove that the project was completed by the company where you work, it would be better to have the workers wearing their uniforms with the name/emblem of the company written on it.

11- For any reason, whenever there is a need to take a photograph of any well-known object that may not indicate its size in the photograph, or may vary in size like a hole in the street or an unfamiliar object, it would be much better to include in the picture another object with a known size, such as a pencil, a ruler, or even a person of a typical height/size. Everyone feels the need for such comparative object in pictures. This event is most observed during shopping through the internet, where you may see something that looks beautiful and large in the picture, and when you receive it, you may be surprised to find that it is a tiny thing, and vice versa.

12- Economy is the life-blood of nearly all professions. From the technical point of view, it is quite possible to go to the moon, but the genius thing is to make it affordable. All professions aim to submit their services to people with the minimum possible cost without concessions regarding the quality. Having said that, it is recommended that new graduates pay attention to the economic side of whatever work they are involved in at least as much as than they do regarding the quality and safety matters. Many professionals simply say they are not economists. This may be true to some limit; however, they must be in continuous touch and coordination with professional economists regarding how to reduce the cost and shorten the period required for the completion of the relevant woks without affecting the required quality. When there is a bid for any project, following the required specifications of the project that is proposed for execution, the bidder that offers the lowest cost and shortest period is most likely to be the winner.

13- If you work as a manager and you need to give a part of the works to a sub-contractor (or to a foreman), then, you should not give any payment in advance before the work starts, or else, that sub-contractor is likely to take the money and just disappear. Afterwards, you need to nearly beg them to start the works, and usually receive no reaction. The amount of payment given to the sub-contractor must be equal to the value of the completed works at every stage and never more.

14- When there are some work-relevant materials to be purchased, it would be better if you accompany the sub-contractor (or a foreman) during the selection and purchase stages. It is also commonly observed that when you agree with an experienced sub-contractor to perform some works, you may be surprised to see the required works being performed by a sub-sub-contractor and/or given to an inexperienced young ones (even children) to do the job without any supervision. In order to minimize the occurrence of such events, you must include these conditions clearly regarding this matter into the contract you sign.

7.3. Signing Documents

Frequently, you need to sign documents of different kinds at work. It is receommended to pay attention to the following situations:

1- Even if you are in extreme hurry and have no time to write an urgent document or letter, never make the most dangerous mistake of your life in putting your signature on a blank paper and submit it to someone else in order to complete the required text later on. Such action is extremely dangerous. This is because, with your signature on a blank paper, anything at all may be written by the other person and destroys your life. In case of the feared event happens, the court can never help you about it even if everyone knows that you are innocent.

2- After you sign a document that contains a statement, in order to minimize the risk of someone adding new unwanted sentences after you sign the document, it is always recommended to add the date of your signature just after the end of the last paragraph of the statement, or, that you put your signature at the same location. Either the date or your signature at the end of the last paragraph should indicate the end of the statement.

3- When receiving a document that contains the list of items, make sure that the document/list satisfies the following standard conditions:

   a- The blank lines below the last line of the items explained in the list must be crossed with permanent pen. If you see that space not being crossed, then, you cross it by hand writing or by using a ruler.

   b- Make sure that the number of items in the list given for signature, the financial numbers, and the grand total value of all items is written in both numbers and words.

   c- Sign only after making sure the required materials are received (or sent) and never before that. It may be better if someone else who helped in receiving the goods sign next to your signature.

   d- There must be two copies of whatever you sign, one for you to be kept in your archives and the other to be given to the other side. If only one copy comes to you to sign it and then be taken away, then, after signing it, take a photocopy or even a photograph by the mobile of the document and store it in your data-base. Never feel shy about doing that even if others felt uncomfortable and/or find it like a "lack of trust."

4- No matter how tired you may be and/or how many documents you have to sign, you really must make sure that you sign nothing without checking the contents. Otherwise, it is extremely dangerous to sign without looking. Also, do not forget to check that the date of the document is written, and if not so, write it by hand next to your signature. If the date shown on the submitted document appears to be different from the date of the document submitted to you, then, write by hand the real new date next to your signature.

5- The precautions explained previously for having a copy for yourself of anything you sign is extremely essential simply because, although in rare cases, if someone forges the documents you already signed and put you in trouble, then, your stored copies would be the only way to prove your innocence. Whether these copies are little in number or too many, you need to classify them according to the subject and date, and store them as hardware as well as software at your work place with software backups on flash memory or external hard disk kept at home. In case anyone shows discomfort about your being specific and careful regarding these matters, try to answer them calmly by saying: (a) the matter is not personal at all; (b) the court is full of disputes between sides regarding such matters; (c) this is just a normal procedure to be continuously followed; (d) such documents will be delivered to and processed through different offices and not be given to one single person. If the other side insists that you should not do whatever recommended in that section, this should indicate that he has some mean aims in fiddling with such documents. If you ask him why he is feeling uncomfortable and insisting on his opinion, he is likely to accept your way simply because it is no logic or legal explanation for his request. The reader should remember that such events are common everywhere with different severity.

7.4. Working Abroad

Working abroad, as explained previously in Chapter 4, is one of the choices that may suit the condition of some graduates. However, it is good to consider the information, recommendations and precautions explained in the following paragraphs.

1- Before leaving your native country, photocopy your ID, your passport and driving license. After that, have them translated through a sworn translator, and get them approved by the Public Notary both in your native country as well as in the host country after being there. Keep these approved photocopies with you all time. After you arrive to the host country, some companies may take your passport and keep it in a safe. In fact, if the company does that, it is not a good sign due to several reasons such as you would have no identity or passport to be presented in case of a need somewhere, particularly if you are alone. Worse than that is in case of any dispute between you and the company and you decide to go back home, the company may prevent you from returning home by holding your passport.

2- Never take/accept anything at all from others in the airport no matter how little or simple it may look like. Among such things, offering you a souvenir, or just asking you to share their load of baggage in case they claim to have more weight than the allowed limits. You never know what may be hidden inside such things no matter how simple and innocent they may look like. After all, it is good to remember that drug smugglers are professional in that dirty business. Frequently, there are crooks in airports in all over the world with good appearance in order to fool others as being business men that can be trusted. Even if they give you their address and cards (may be a false or non-existing name and address), do not give your address or other information about yourself, particularly when they seem to be curious about you and ask you questions that seem to be more than normal.

3- Learning at least the basic of the language of the host country as quickly as possible is one of the essential conditions to minimize the risks involved during your stay over there. This is also important in order to improve your productivity at work and as well as to minimize your loneliness during that period.

4- During learning and practicing the new language of the host country, particularly if it is a developing one, you may come across a situation that may upset you, or even put you off learning that language altogether. In other words, you might see the person/s you talk to suddenly burst in laughing at your linguistic mistakes even during the discussion of a serious matter. This is a situation that you need to be patient about for a long time until your language gets better. Generally speaking, despite that the other person/s is likely to have laughed at the way you talk with good intention, such behavior is likely to make you feel uncomfortable and discourage from going on in your talk. Only few may swallow this unpleasant situation while the majority is likely to feel offended and stop talking, and even decide to stop learning that language. Laughing this way on the other person's linguistic mistakes (grammatical, pronunciation, and/or using the wrong words) is a clear indication of being primitive and of the lack of self-control.

5- When you decide to learn the language of the country where you work, try not to catch the local accent. Try to learn the formal language with no accent. The best source to apply this is to concentrate on some specific programs on the TV such as the news and scientific programs. Moreover, if you always stick to your friends at work from your native country, you are likely to be slow in learning the new language.

6- Do not walk alone in the evening, particularly in empty streets. When being a foreigner, you are more vulnerable, particularly when coming across gangs which prefer dark and empty streets. In a developed country, three dear friends of mine (two specialized medical doctors and one senior engineer: three brothers) went for a walk near the hospital where one of the two doctors used to work. They came under sever attack by a group of drunken local citizens. They suffered broken legs and ribs. Saving them took a long time because there was only one single policewoman on site and needed reinforcement. Eventually, the three friends were covered in blood and taken on stretchers to the same nearby hospital where that doctor used to work. Their only sin was being foreigners in the wrong place and wrong time. The three brothers have white complexion and blue eyes but the attackers detected their being foreigners from their accent. Another bitter incident is relevant to my relative (a senior judge), during his visit to his son in one of the largest cities in a developed country, he did the same mistake in going for an evening walk in a busy street. Suddenly, he was pulled to a narrow side street by a gang, and was robbed and beaten viciously. He spent about a couple of weeks in a hospital after which he traveled to his country. He died nearly one month later due to his injuries. There are more incidents of such kind relevant to several of dear friends and even relatives with no space to explain their ordeals in this concise book. Briefly, the precaution explained in this section is recommended to be taken seriously because darkness is the best cover for outlaws, particularly when streets are not crowded.

7- Minimize traveling alone in your car for long distances such as between cities. If necessary, try to travel with a friend during the day time when the traffic is relatively more active. Some years ago, I attended the funeral of a friend. His family said that he passed away due to a heart attack. However, after nearly a month from that incident, I learned that this friend was working abroad and was found dead on the side of the road between two cities after being robbed of his money and both kidneys. Very likely only drug addicts would do such a vicious thing. The interesting thing is that drug addicts, even after a short period of doing any horrible act, may not remember anything about what they did.

8- In a foreign country, do not make quick friendships with persons that you never knew before. Most people everywhere in the world are good and friendly; however, it is essential to remember that while being abroad, one is relatively more vulnerable towards being cheated and/or attacked.

9- Do not criticize the host country even when a friend of that country criticizes it. Also, try to follow the recommendation given in Paragraph 7.1.29 particularly when being abroad. Do not do that even while talking with non-natives like you. Remember that no one forced you to go and work in that country where life may not be comfortable for you in different aspects.

10- As explained in Chapter 4, Paragraph 4.4.2.g, during your stay abroad, you may come across individuals that seem to be very friendly and rush to help you in every aspect of your life over there. Such persons may be sincere in their friendship and wish to help; however, some others may be trying to indirectly attract you to their group or organization. This process is usually slow and implicit. In case you feel that they are trying to drag you into their organization, try to be gentle in rejecting the matter due to any reason you may think of, such as being too busy and the like. If you rejection is conveyed in a rough manner, they may try to harm you somehow. Particularly when being abroad, ambitious and innocent young graduates represent the best prey for such organizations. Their aims may vary from pushing you to spy on your own country to drug trafficking or even terrorism. Usually, they are powerful, well trained, organized and camouflaged as being educated and gentle citizens. Never think of adventuring in joining such organizations simply because once you join them, it is extremely dangerous to defect. This is simply because you learned their secrets.

11- When being abroad, try to avoid giving your home address to others. Some may think to use it as a declaration of a place they wish to stay in your country (claiming that you are a friend that invited them), and thus, get a visa to your country without your knowledge. Although such cases are rare, but when happens, the arrival/s are unlikely to come to your native country for good purposes, and eventually, you may be in trouble for them using your name and address to enter your country. A funny short story about such situation is about some Bedouin (Arab tribes who have historically inhabited the desert regions in the Arabian Peninsula) saw a dog running like hell and extremely scared. They asked him: what are you afraid of? He said: they are slaughtering all camels over there. They said: but you are a dog and not a camel? He said: until they realize that I am not a camel, it may be too late for me! This may be funny but has a strong meaning about innocent people getting lost and being harmed in some chaotic situations. Therefore, if you are abroad and asked to give your home address, simply give your e-mail address (may be your mobile number too) and say that you have no current address at home because you used to rent a flat that time.

12- During your stay abroad for a long period, there is always the possibility of getting to know a friend of the other sex and thinking of getting married. Your parents are likely not to feel happy about this idea because you are likely to be away from them probably for good, and also for not knowing anything about the background of the one you wish to marry. Moreover, there is no way they can communicate with her/him due to the language barrier. However, you may insist in saying that it is your life and your decision. In such case, it would be good to remember that such marriage has advantages and disadvantages. The main disadvantage is that you are likely to spend most of your life swinging between your native country and the country of your spouse. This is likely to consume nearly all your holidays as well as your money. Frequently, and after the elapse of some time, a dispute between the couple may arise due to each side insisting on getting settled in his/her own country. When being grownups, your children may be confused regarding which culture and/or religion to follow, where to get settled and work, and the like of such difficult decisions. If the dispute between the couple reaches the stage of divorce, then, it is nearly certain that the parents of each of the couple will say that we told you that you were wrong in selecting your spouse from abroad. In fact, the same comments from the parents of each of the couple are likely to be encountered even when one gets married from a partner selected from the same country but from different region, religion or even ethnic minority. Obviously, in this section, explaining some of the disadvantages of such marriage does never mean that it is not recommended. This is simply because there are many successful marriages of such kind. In fact, it is proven scientifically that mixed marriage from different countries is likely to give births to healthier, more intelligent and more beautiful children. In case you decide to go for such marriage, being financially independent from your parents and your parents in law increases the chance of leading a successful marriage. When being abroad, detecting the background and past of your future spouse may be relatively difficult for you as a foreigner in the other country. However, it is common everywhere in the world that good and respected families have good and successful children and vice versa. Obviously, there are exceptions that should not be neglected, but they do not change the general trend.

It may good to remember at an early stage that, generally speaking, children of parents from two different countries wish to live, study and work in the relatively more developed country, which is a natural decision; after all, it is their lives and their future.

13- Due to the fact that the salaries of those who work abroad are likely to be more than what the employees need for their daily expenses. Some companies ask their employees to save their surplus money with the accountant of the company. This is dangerous even if you are given a receipt for that deposited money. If and when the company declares its bankruptcy, your money would be gone with no chance to get it back. In order to minimize such risk, it would be good to transfer your surplus money to your bank account in your native country.

14- In the host country, particularly when being lonely, some may encourage you to "adventure" in using drugs in order to relax and have fun. Unfortunately, drug use seems to be on the increase both in developed and developing countries alike. It is unfortunate that some developed countries seem to show tendency of relaxation regarding this matter, and even making the personal usage of drugs legal. I wish to warn those who may be exposed to such offer. Trying drugs only once will certainly lead to being addicted from the first time/dose, and afterwards, there is no way out of this hell, and there is nothing such as an adventure in or trying it only once. Drug sellers always offer the first dose for free, simply because they know well that one single dose would be enough to trap the buyer and make him beg for the following one/s. Consequently, it would be easy to either sell him much more later on, or, force him to work in selling drugs on behalf of the relevant gang with a salary composed of some doses of the same drug. Even if a friend offers a dose of drug (cannot be called a friend for doing this), the aim of his offer is unlikely for to make you happy. In fact, his main aim, as explained in Chapter 3 – Paragraph 10, is likely to make him feel less guilty when many others make the same mistake.

15- As explained in the previous paragraph, the same may be said about gambling. Usually, those who fall in these extremely dangerous traps disappear from the arena of life and social relations, simply because they lose everything within a short period of time, such as their family, position, money, respect and the like. Also, they tend to be shy for their naive behavior for falling in such traps which are well known to everyone for being dangerous.

16- If you are from a developing country, during your stay/study/work abroad in a developed country, you may come across some unpleasant events that come from some unpleasant people. In fact, and as explained previously, there are good and bad people everywhere including developed countries. Such events may be like in others asking some humiliating questions. In different occasions and different times, I was asked: do you have cars at home? Do you have a post office at home? In fact, sometimes, it may be difficult to distinguish whether those questions are asked with the aim of humiliation or due to real lack of knowledge for being influenced by what they see on the TV and movies. However, when hearing such question, it is really difficult not to answer in a sarcastic way. In relevance to the car question, I said that at home, camels are the only mean for transportation with plate number stuck on its rear end. Also, in relevance to the post office question, my reply was that at home, pigeons are the only way for communications. In both occasions, after the other side felt my being offended, he said that the questions were just a joke. Obviously, they were never pleasant jokes.

Another interesting incident is relevant to one of my friends during his flight through one of the most famous airway companies. He was asked by a hostess: do you prefer a normal meal or the Khomeini one (meaning a meal with no pork)? Obviously, my friend was offended and shocked despite not being an Iranian citizen, but did not complain due to his suspicion that the administration of the airway company is likely to think and behave in the same way as of that hostess, otherwise, she would not get the courage to be so offensive.

While being in the U.K., I was asked by an English friend: "In your country, you drive on the wrong side of the road, don't you?" Unfortunately, as a reflex, my answer was: "Yes, we do, sorry about that!" Later on, I felt sorry and guilty for the giving such sarcastic answer, simply because that friend is likely to have used that term of "driving on the wrong side of the road" for being a common one in the U.K. without any intention of being offensive.

Obviously, the term "driving on the wrong side of the road" has an implicit arrogance which indirectly means that anything different from the traffic system in the U.K. is wrong. Also, the unpleasant behavior of that hostess may have been due to being separated from her foreign x-boyfriend (or husband) and left with bitter memories, which eventually led to her hating all foreigners.

Most people tend to generalize in their reaction after a minor unpleasant event caused by one individual or more. Sometimes, a general negative reaction may be generated by the native people due to their city being too crowded by foreigners. In such case, it would be fair to say that this situation could be really irritating to the native people due to the existence of different cultures, and also, due to the difficulties encountered regarding communication and security aspects of life. Having said that may be best expressed by that interesting and funny caricature which I found in an English magazine. The drawing shows two foreigners (non-English) walking in the center of London next to BigBen. One of them said to the other: London is really a beautiful city, and I like it very much; however, the only problem of this city is that there are so many English people in it!

When being abroad anywhere, even if being offended in some occasions like those explained in the previous paragraphs, one should be calm and try not to react negatively in a generalized way towards all people in that country. This is simply because those unpleasant individuals are only a primitive minority, and they never represent their country in anyway. Do not forget that everybody in those so-called developed countries is not so developed and/or well informed about the real situation in developing countries. This section is presented to those that may be too sensitive towards such unpleasant events with the aim of encouraging them to be calm and forgiving. After all, we never selected our place of birth, name, gender, parents, language, religion, color, physical appearance, and the surrounding social and economic environment. We all are citizens of the lonely planet earth, and we must manage to live peacefuly together in it.

Chapter 8 Conclusion

The joy of completing the writing of this book was great. It was really like paying back my debt for my being lucky in getting access to good education, and also, for being in continuous touch with my wonderful students who are the most innocent and capable section in society. After all, they are the future of this world.

If the contents of this book appear to be useful even to a fraction of the readers, that would be still very rewarding to me. For most of the readers being young and inexperienced in life, some sections in it may be boring to them for being relatively classical. However, as during listening to music and/or watching films, when listening/watching is repeated, there is always something new to feel and see which was not noticed previously. The same with this book, it may take some time intervals and/or encountering some events in order to see its usefulness. Only then, the reader may be more interested to review it yet again.

I expect that most of my colleagues at work, and probably most academics in other universities, share me my thoughts. However, the missing thing here is to gather those thoughts and put them in such a concise book so that both students and graduates can access them easily at any time.

It is not enough to know the thing whatever it is, in fact, it is everybody's duty to convey that knowledge to others in order to save them the time required to find it and learn it as early as possible. The best way to enable the access of knowledge in a convenient way is through writing a book. In recent times, free e-books and photocopying books reduced the expected financial profits to nearly zero. The only aim left nowadays is purely to spread information freely and let others benefit from it.

It may be better if, for each university, and preferably even for each faculty, there would be an advisory service office led by an experienced staff that is capable of performing better than what this book can do. Obviously, such service will have long term positive advantages for all students. Despite the expected extra financial cost on any university that employs such staff, it is certain that the existence of such office would improve the reputation of the university as well as in guiding students and graduates to the optimum direction towards a better future. Similar counseling offices usually exist in most of the universities in developed countries, but their services are limited to assisting students in finding accommodation, solving their financial, health, legal, personal problems, and the like. These services do not include the advice needed for students and graduates regarding what to do afterwards according to the specific circumstances of each student. It is interesting that in most schools, such advisory staff exists and usually very active in helping to guide students regarding the difficulties encountered in and outside the school, while in most universities the idea of employing such staff is not taken seriously yet.

Finaly, I wish to thank the readers for evaluating my thoughts, and I welcome any criticizm and/or proposal regarding the contents of this book. Your feed-back may be sent to my E-mail address: mazenkavvas@gmail.com. Please notice that in my surname, there are two consequtive "v"s and not one "w".

www.ingramcontent.com/pod-product-compliance
Lightning Source LLC
Chambersburg PA
CBHW060839190426
43197CB00040B/2705